John Brookfield

TRAINING
with
CABLES
for
STRENGTH

IronMind Enterprises, Inc.
Nevada City, California

Training with Cables for Strength
by John Brookfield

Copyright© 2001 IronMind Enterprises, Inc.

Cataloguing in Publication Data
Brookfield, John—
Training with cables for strength
1. Weight training 2. Fitness and health   I. Title
2001   796.41   2001-131923
0-926888-10-2

Published in the United States of America
IronMind Enterprises, Inc., P. O. Box 1228, Nevada City, CA 95959 USA

Book and cover design by
Tony Agpoon, San Francisco, California

Photos by Terry Jarrell, except as follows: photos on pages 42, 52, 65, 70 and 75 by Angela Beckman.

To my daughter Heather

John Brookfield and daughter Heather, age four.

About the Author

One day, a little over a decade ago, I got a call from someone named John Brookfield, who introduced himself as a professional strongman. John said he had heard that we sold heavy-duty hand grippers, and since he was something of a grip specialist, and had set the goal for himself of developing the world's strongest set of hands, he wanted to get some of our grippers. John went on to become the second person in the world we officially recognized as having closed our No. 3 Captains of Crush® gripper, but much more than that, he has established himself in our minds as a foremost authority on grip training. Of course, John is no armchair expert, as he comfortably inhabits the top echelons in the principal forms of grip strength, and without question, he also has uncanny wrist strength: quite simply, John is the best in the world that we know of when it comes to bending short objects, such as spikes. John has put on countless shows in his professional strongman career, and in a field that has had more than one charlatan, John is the real McCoy.

Despite all of his accomplishments in the strength world, there are three other things that immediately come to mind when I think of John Brookfield. First, John is absolutely one of the most creative minds you will ever run into when it comes to grip training, and while some people are content to pursue a monkey-see-monkey-do approach, or to gripe instead of grip, or to talk instead of train, John is always out there developing something new and is steadily training, training, training. This passion, we have always felt, is one of the real secrets to John's success, and through this book on cable training, as he did with *Mastery of Hand Strength*, John will share many of his ideas with you. When you read *Training with Cables for Strength*, you have a rare chance to learn from someone who knows what he's talking about and who practices what he preaches.

Second, when he comes up with something new, John doesn't require a million dollar budget for his equipment, and I have kidded him that for a guy who gets so much use from duct tape, he should get a fat advertising contract from a big tape manufacturer. The good news here is that you won't have to break your budget to train the Brookfield way, so lack of money will never be an excuse for you.

Third, John has the integrity to admit when he's wrong, as he did about originally saying that it was impossible to burst soda or beer cans, but then realizing that not only could it be done, but he, himself, could become extremely proficient at it. I felt this spoke volumes about John's character, and made it even easier for us to tip our hats in John's direction.

Pull up a chair and make yourself comfortable, because as we've always said, John will make you feel as if you're sitting around the kitchen table talking to him, and get ready to put some of his tips to work in your own training.

Best of luck.

Randall J. Strossen, Ph.D.
President
IronMind Enterprises, Inc.
Nevada City, California

Other IronMind Enterprises, Inc. Publications:

SUPER SQUATS: How to Gain 30 Pounds of Muscle in 6 Weeks
   by Randall J. Strossen, Ph.D.

The Complete Keys to Progress
   by John McCallum, edited by Randall J. Strossen, Ph.D.

Mastery of Hand Strength
   by John Brookfield

IronMind: Stronger Minds, Stronger Bodies
   by Randall J. Strossen, Ph.D.

MILO: A Journal for Serious Strength Athletes,
   Randall J. Strossen, Ph.D., Publisher and Editor-in-chief

Powerlifting Basics, Texas-style: The Adventures of Lope Delk
   by Paul Kelso

Of Stones and Strength
   by Steve Jeck and Peter Martin

IronMind Training Tablet No. 1
   by Randall J. Strossen, Ph.D.

IronMind Training Tablet No. 2
   by Randall J. Strossen, Ph.D.

Sons of Samson, Volume 2 Profiles
   by David Webster

Rock, Iron, Steel: The Book of Strength
   by Steve Justa

Paul Anderson: The Mightiest Minister
   by Randall J. Strossen, Ph.D.

The Strongest Man in History: Louis Cyr, Amazing Canadian
   by Ben Weider

To order additional copies of *Training with Cables for Strength* or for
a catalog of IronMind Enterprises, Inc. publications and products,
please contact:

   IronMind Enterprises, Inc.
   P. O. Box 1228
   Nevada City, CA 95959 USA
   tel: (530) 265-6725
   fax: (530) 265-4876
   website: www.ironmind.com
   e-mail: sales@ironmind.com

Contents

You can't think about using cables
without thinking about getting stronger.

Chapter 1

Getting Started

Why Cables?

You may ask, why should anyone want to use cables in today's world? After all, there are all kinds of strength training tools available to the would-be champion of today. There are, of course, free weights, as well as all types of weight machines. Some machines of today are even computerized. The other day I visited a fitness facility and looked at all the new computerized bikes and stair-climbers. As I walked through the building I came upon a large room with a sign on the door that read Strength Training. Inside, I saw what is known as the latest in resistance training: all types of computerized machines with buttons and panels with all kinds of lights. While selecting a machine to try out, I noticed a large sign on the wall saying all members must be properly instructed before using the equipment. I thought to myself, how could these machines stump a mental giant like myself? After all, these new machines couldn't be any harder than flying a spaceship, could they?

My point is not that these machines don't have their place in today's society, because anyone who has ever trained for anything from football to tennis knows that any kind of resistance has some positive effect on the muscles. However, in today's scientific world, I think we have gotten away from the basic principles, or the foundation, for success, not only in strength but in life itself. We look to the glitter and fancy, instead of the true answer.

We are starting to see in athletics a return to the basics, or the simple solution, to gain usable strength. Coaches and athletes alike are returning to good old weightlifting exercises, like power cleans, squats, and bent over rows. Exercises like these are great for developing true strength, the kind that can be used on the football field or for throwing the shot put. Of course, another advantage free weights have over machines is that you must balance the bar yourself, unlike with machines, which are balanced for you.

You are probably wondering by now why this section is entitled "Why Cables?" Very simply, cables should be a prime part of any athlete's training program for several reasons. One is that cables increase flexibility dramatically. We will discuss the advantages of cables for increasing flexibility later.

Let's look at the strength advantages of cables. I know that cables have not been taken very seriously for the simple fact that everyone still remembers the cables he saw in his local sporting goods store when he was in junior high school. You know, the ones that Aunt Betsy could pull for ten good repetitions the first time she put her hands on them. Unfortunately there are cheap cable sets in sporting goods stores and department stores around the country, and for this reason, cables have not been taken seriously as a strength developer.

The type of cables I'm talking about is the type used in Europe many years ago. You will still see these cables used in Europe, but not as often as in the past. They are able to challenge the strongest of men. A good set of cables allows anyone from the weakest to the strongest to progress by adding cables. Adding cables, of course, works on basic strength through the progressive resistance principle. With this point in mind, you can develop every part of the body to its utmost with cables.

You have probably wondered how you can train the lower body with cables. In Chapter 3, Cable Exercises, this will be discussed in depth. For now, let's look at why cables are a great asset to the athlete.

For a basic understanding, let's consider free weight exercises. As useful as they are, the main disadvantage is that the weight or resistance is always going down or toward the ground. This, of course, is basic gravity in action. Now, many of you are probably already wondering, what's wrong with the weight or resistance pulling toward the ground? In many circumstances, nothing; in fact, it is important to train with some exercises where the resistance is toward the ground. However, let's look at some activities where the resistance isn't downwards.

In a wrestling match, for example, the resistance comes from all angles. Whether you're on the mat or standing up grappling, the resistance is very rarely pulling down, as it is with weights. This is the reason that wrestlers of the past used cable pulling as a large part of their training. Many wrestlers and strongmen of the past used to say that cables were better than weights for developing usable strength. Usable strength is essential for sports or activities requiring a large output of strength, such as wrestling, arm wrestling, shot putting, rock climbing, swimming, etc.

Once again, remember that in these sports and countless others, the resistance is not always toward the ground. In swimming, for instance, the force required is very different from weights, and the exertion and the force are much more like cable pulling. Wrestling and swimming are just two examples, and the list could go on. My point is not that weights aren't good, but they are limited for some activities.

You may ask me, then, why are not a lot more athletes using cables in their routines? The answer is very simple. There are very, very few athletes who know about the true use of cables, and there is also not much information on cables in the market today. I know that if more people started training with cables, they would quickly see the advantages. I am not saying to quit lifting weights—I'm saying if you use cables along with your weight training, you will get great results and climb to a high level of strength that can be used for any sport or activity inside or outside the weight room.

Flexibility

We mentioned increased flexibility earlier as a result of pulling cables. The rotation of the shoulders is dramatically improved by many cable exercises. My own shoulders have increased their range of motion from all angles, and as a result, my shoulder strength has gained. I will give you an example. As a professional strongman, I bend a lot of bars behind my neck, in programs as well as in practice. One of my challenge feats I've used for years is bending very short steel bars behind my neck. I have had many of the strongest try to bend these short bars without any luck. The reason for this is that despite their great upper body strength, they are put into a position where they cannot exert much of their power because they are out of their power zone. They are in a position where they have no flexibility, thus reducing their strength dramatically. I found out myself that the more I used cables, the shorter and stronger bars I could bend in this position.

Let's look at the back pressout as another example. In this cable exercise, your cables are behind your mid back and your hands are at your sides grasping the handles. The object is to push outward away from your body and stretch the cables so that your arms are completely straight out at your sides and your elbows are locked. This exercise is one example of how flexibility is gained through cables. A couple of years ago I had a few friends of mine who were powerlifters try a few cable exercises. Two of the three lifters could not even get their arms into position to do the back pressout, and the other could get in the right position, but felt that he had little strength for the press because the angle decreased his flexibility. These gentlemen quickly found out that when they got a little out of their element, they were at a loss.

This goes back to my earlier point about usable strength. When cables become a part of a person's training program, the trainee is challenged with resistance from every angle possible. This resistance comes from the sides, up, diagonally, and down, and combinations of directions. These different angles of resistance are the same ones you experience in real-life activities, like wrestling, archery, boxing, and swimming. All these cable exercises increase your strength levels from every angle and every line of pull. You will gain strength and flexibility in your shoulders, arms, back, and neck, and even your legs. You will start gaining strength for any task or activity, and you will be strong from every angle.

Another advantage of cables is that the farther they stretch, the greater the resistance. With free weights and machines, the lock-out, or the final exertion of the motion, is done with the same amount of weight or resistance. However, the lock-out with cables involves greater resistance due to the stretching or expanding of the cables. This develops strength throughout the entire motion. Once again, you will find this type of resistance more practical for real-life activities.

Cables also develop the tendons and ligaments in a very special way, because the resistance comes from every angle, unlike other types of strength training. I have done different types of cable pulling for years, and I noticed that at the times when I neglected my cable exercises, I was much more prone to pulling muscles. I didn't feel as flexible or toned, particularly in my shoulders. However, the more cable exercises I included in my routine, the stronger and more confident I felt during heavy exertion, either in sports or weight training.

Another important point in regard to cable pulling is that with cables, the pressure or resistance put on the muscles is consistent; in other words, it is steady throughout the pull. There is no lull or reduction of resistance that takes place throughout the exercise, so the muscles as well as the tendons and ligaments get the ultimate workout. This type of workout, along with progressive resistance, is the most productive training method ever.

If you use cable exercises along with your weight training exercises, you not only will experience great gains in strength and performance, you will also have more longevity in your training and sports due to increased flexibility and stronger tendons and ligaments.

Massage and Relaxation

I feel it is important to briefly discuss the benefits of massage and other methods that will help you relax and remove lactic acid, by improving circulation. I had never been big on massage until the last couple of years. I have found that a good massage helps you gain strength by improving circulation. When you do heavy strength training, you tend to build up a lot of lactic acid, which decreases blood flow or circulation. Over a period of time, your muscles can feel a little tight or a little sore. When this is the case, you can hit a sticking point in your exercise. You may have a hard time making strength gains, or perhaps you may feel a little sluggish or less explosive. If you're trying to gain size, you may experience a standstill in growth in your measurements.

I have myself been in this situation on many occasions and found that a good massage made all the difference in the world. After the massage I felt much fresher, and I also found out that my strength jumped up much more rapidly. The reason for this is the increased circulation. This feeling will also give you a better outlook and keep you motivated.

I know by now that you're saying to yourself that massage therapists are expensive. This is true, and the majority of you out there may not be able to afford massages on a regular basis. To be honest with you, I can't either, so I try to get a massage before I feel myself getting burned out or stale. I know of many people who get several massages a week and swear by it. However, I have found that a massage about every two or three weeks is sufficient to keep the circulation going properly. If you can't afford a massage every few weeks, or you don't have access to a massage therapist, here are a couple of other alternatives.

First of all, let's not forget the benefits of the whirlpool or Jacuzzi. They relax our bodies and our minds. They are soothing in a very special way. To get the maximum benefit out of this method, you will want to position yourself so that the jet spray is spraying out on you and massaging your muscles. Try to move into positions so that every muscle gets this massaging effect. This will also help circulation and remove lactic acid build-up.

Here is another method you may use to help circulation and reduce lactic acid build-up if you don't have access to a whirlpool at a local health club. The mineral salts bath is very helpful and also convenient. You can relax in a hot bath in the convenience of your own home. Adding the mineral salts to your hot bath water will help your circulation, as well as help relax tired muscles. This type of bath is good therapy for a weary mind, and let's not forget that the mind and body go together.

I strongly urge you to try some of these circulation enhancers, if not all of them. They will help you achieve your goals in the world of size and strength, and enhance your athletic performance.

Cables for Travel

When it comes to being on the road, cables can't be beat; they can be transported anywhere. Just think, what else can you carry wherever you go that has unlimited resistance in any exercise. You can carry cables on an airplane, a train, or even on a long bicycle trip. They can be put into your suitcase, gym bag, or shaving kit. You can pick a resistance of a few pounds or a resistance of a few hundred pounds.

Cables can be used by an out-of-shape couch potato, or they can be used by the world's strongest man. They will enhance the strength and flexibility of any athlete in any sport. I could go on and on about the advantages of cables, but the bottom line is, you can't think about using cables without thinking about getting stronger.

Chapter 2

The History of Cables

Bow and Arrow

Exercising with cables can be traced way back in time. One example of this is early hunters with their bows and arrows. The bows were, of course, used to hunt for survival, but they were also used for exercise. The bow functions similarly to cables, applying the same type of resistance. The earlier bows were different from most of the bows of today. The modern-day compound bow has taken over the archery world. These modern compounds use the weight let-off principle, which allows the archer to hold less weight in the shooting or fully drawn position.

The bows of the past were longbows and recurve models and held the same resistance throughout the entire movement. The result was stronger muscles.

I recall reading in folklore of long ago how different heroes had competitions to see who could pull a certain bow back the most times, or how certain men of might had bows that were said to be impossible to draw except by themselves. Bows have always been a symbol of strength throughout the world.

I myself have a specially made longbow that requires 160 pounds of pressure to fully draw. This bow is supposed to be the second strongest known bow there is. The strongest is a longbow that is listed in the *Guinness Book of Records*, said to require 172 pounds of pressure to fully draw. To some of you out there who don't know much about archery, this may not sound like much. However, bows like these are more than a handful to draw. You could spend many months vainly looking for someone who could pull such a bow.

Only through years of pulling cables and different types of gadgets that work on the same principle, have I been able to handle my 160-pound bow. The stress this bow puts on my shoulder is unbelievable. As you can see, the bow can be used not only for hunting, but also as a strength and endurance tool.

Pulling Inner Tubes

Another form of cable pulling that has been popular through the years is pulling inner tubes. I have seen and heard of inner tubes being pulled in a couple of different ways.

A popular training tool for judo is pulling different-sized inner tubes to simulate different throws. This is done by hooking the tubes to the wall or around a small tree. From here, the student grasps the tubes with one end in each hand and pulls the tubes the same way he would pull against an opponent in attempting to throw him. As the student gets stronger, he either adds another tube or uses a larger, thicker tube. It is amazing how much pulling strength can be developed in this manner as you continue to use greater resistance.

Years ago I was heavily involved in judo, as well as some other grappling arts. Shortly after I began to train seriously, I was introduced to this style of inner tube pulling. In the evening I would train by wrapping heavy inner tubes around a small tree trunk and pulling these tubes toward me in ways that would simulate pulling an opponent toward me to be thrown. First of all, this improved my throwing techniques by leaps and bounds, but what I also noticed is that I became much stronger from all the heavy inner tube pulling. I began to use heavier tubes and increase my workout time. Before I knew it, I was doing about two thousand repetitions with the tubes. I was feeling stronger and fitter than ever.

An old Japanese gentleman I used to know trained in this same fashion. He was a former world judo champion. Of course he spent hours training on the mat with different judo players, but when he didn't have the chance to train with partners, he would go into his backyard and pull on inner tubes. As mentioned before, he would simulate the different judo throws by pulling on the tubes in the same manner he would pull and throw an opponent. At one particular point in his life, the studio where he instructed and trained had closed down. There was not another judo school within driving distance, so he used these inner tubes to maintain good muscle tone and to keep his throwing techniques as sharp as he could, without having any partners.

Over a period of time, he got up to an unbelievable seven thousand repetitions a day. This is absolutely incredible. The most amazing thing about this was his strength gains. I worked out with him a few times in his backyard, and I was amazed at how strong he had become on this program. He wasn't a big man, but he was wiry. He was very hard to throw and also very strong on the mat. I can honestly say that this gentleman was the most deceptively strong person that I have ever encountered. All of his strength came from pulling his version of cables, which were ordinary inner tubes. Bicycle inner tubes, as well as stronger motorcycle tubes, are great for pulling.

Pullers of Old

My intentions for this book are to tell you the advantages of cables and to provide a complete guide to using cables for muscle building and sports of all kinds. However, this book would not be complete if a few greats of old were not mentioned.

First of all, let's look at Eugen Sandow. Sandow, born in East Prussia, was one of the most famous strongmen of all time. Sandow was known for his good looks and great personality as much as for his strength and athletic ability. He excelled in all types of lifting and strength feats. Cable pulling, or strand pulling as it is often called, was one of his specialties. Sandow played a huge role in the promotion of cable pulling. Many would-be champions, young and old alike, started pulling cables because they saw or heard of Sandow pulling cables as part of his daily exercise. The military even had their soldiers working out on cable exercises because of Sandow's influence.

Sandow had a wall unit that he sold called Sandow's Own Combined Developer. This developer was a device that hooked to a door or to the wall and enabled you to stretch cables in many directions and do a variety of exercises. Reports showed that this unit was highly productive, with many pupils showing great results. Eugen Sandow was a true pioneer, not only for cable training, but for physical fitness in general.

Another notable strongman who excelled at cable pulling was the great Thomas Inch of Great Britain. Inch's long career as a strongman was amazing. He performed his first act at the age of sixteen years; included in his act was a strong set of cables. Inch continued to improve on his cable pulling. He had many challenge feats, throughout the years, in which cables were involved, one of which was to pull a heavy set of cables all the way out in the front chest pull position, while a 56-pound weight hung from the little finger of each hand. This was an amazing feat of strength and must be tried to truly appreciate the difficulty.

Inch excelled at all types of cable pulling. He was very thick in build, but very flexible. Much of his flexibility was due to consistent use of cables throughout the years. He performed his strength act until he was seventy years of age and continued to train up to ninety.

Fred Rollon of Germany billed himself as the world's greatest strand, or cable, puller, and his act consisted mostly of cable pulling. He used a set of cables which he stated could resist the pull of horses. This was a bold statement, and lucky for him, there were people in his audience and not horses. On several occasions he was challenged and was forced to lift weights, even though he wasn't really a lifter. However, he did quite well in the overhead lifts and appeared to be a natural in pressing movements. Rollon continued to pull cables throughout his career and developed one of the most impressive backs in history. Most of today's bodybuilders would be happy to have as impressive a back as Rollon had.

Tromp Van Diggelen was a South African strongman with a proud, snobbish attitude. He excelled at cable pulling and offered large amounts of money to anyone who was able to fully stretch his cables. He did a variety of different feats of strength; however, it was always cable pulling which was his challenge feat. He was also the trainer of many strongmen and wrestlers.

The list of noteworthy cable pullers could go on and on, and only a few are mentioned here. In fact, there were quite a few pullers who claimed to be the world's best. This will always be a question mark, and we will never know who was actually the best, because the cables were not checked for accuracy. Also we know, despite the great strength and skill of the strongmen of the past, that at times a certain amount of exaggeration went along with some of their claims.

What we do know is that cable pullers of the past developed very strong athletic builds with great flexibility in their upper bodies due to their cable training. Looking back on these athletes who specialized in cable exercises, we see that the majority of them had long and successful careers.

I guarantee you, if you start a program of one-legged squats, you will notice a great difference in your balance and leg strength when you play any type of sport, whether competitive or leisure.

Chapter 3

Cable Exercises

Starting Tips

It is important to understand the basics of cables before you start. Since cable training is pretty well unknown, there are a few important points to be made. The tips that follow are essential for proper cable training. Please read them and follow them, so your training can be enjoyable as well as productive.

1. My first tip, and probably the most important, is to start with light resistance so that your muscles can get used to the different type of stress that these exercises will put on them. Even if you are a weightlifting or bodybuilding champion, I urge you to progress slowly. While you may feel you can use more cable resistance right from the start, take at least several weeks to get your muscles used to this different type of stress. Also, your flexibility will be enhanced after a few weeks of cable training.

A couple of years ago, I started cable training again after a very long layoff and found out the hard way. Of course, I knew all about cable training so I burst right into heavy resistance. I was very strong at the different movements, and in my mind, thought about unbelievable gains in strength. What I didn't think of was that even though my muscles were strong, they were not used to this type of stress. The result was that after a couple of weeks of big jumps in resistance, I started to experience shoulder pain directly in the deltoid. I continued to train heavily even though my shoulder was tight and somewhat sore. The actual time it took to get my shoulders up to par was about three months; however, I had trouble reaching my goals because of a slight pain in my shoulders. I also had a slight but consistent pain in my lower elbow because of heavy cable pulling. My point is that cable pulling places demands on your upper body you may not be used to.

You will find that if you train smart and start slowly, you will build a foundation that will make you much stronger and more flexible—and much less at risk of getting injured. You, of course, want to add resistance and work on the progressive resistance concept, but once again, start slowly and let your muscles get used to cable pulling.

2. The second tip is to read the instructions carefully in the exercise section. Don't be in too big a hurry to get started. Make sure you understand each exercise before attempting it. You want to get the most out of every movement.

3. My third tip is to look at the photos closely so you can perform the exercises properly. I have found that a mirror is very useful with cable pulling. It will, of course, be useful to the beginner to study his own form, but it will also help the experienced athlete concentrate on the correct form. You will also find a mirror useful to help motivate yourself during your workout.

4. A point that is not usually brought up with any kind of strength training—even though most people understand proper breathing—is to always remember to breathe correctly. Never hold your breath during an exercise. Always breathe naturally. Inhale as you stretch or expand your cables and exhale as you relax them back to the starting position.

5. Don't strain, as we discussed earlier. Your objective is to train and build your body, not injure it. Your strength will consistently grow as you train progressively. Be patient and remember, little by little one goes far.

6. As with any type of training, train each side of your body equally for balanced development.

7. Remember to grip the handles of the cables firmly. Losing your grip, or letting go of the handles, could result in injury, possibly a toothy experience. Also, be sure to keep your foot well within the handle when you're performing exercises where one foot or both feet are placed within the handles.

8. Be sure to grip the handles properly, as illustrated in each exercise. You will notice that the palms may be facing each other (inward) in many exercises, and they may be gripping the handles back to back (outward) in others. Study the photos closely before starting the exercises.

9. My final tip will probably answer a question that a lot of you are wondering about now. That question is, how often should I train and how many exercises and sets should I do?

Well, to answer the first question, I would suggest training every other day, training every body part in the same workout. Many lifters like to do split routines in which they train every day, training different body parts on different days. I feel that you can profit from this type of routine; however, I recommend the every-other-day routine where you train every body part. My reason for this is that cables stress and work your shoulders and upper back muscles to the extreme. I have found through experience that most of the exercises work these muscles much more than any other type of strength training. Therefore, it is better to rest from cable exercises every other day to achieve your maximum gains in size and strength.

As far as how many exercises you should perform, I can tell you once again that cable pulling works your shoulders to their utmost. With this in mind, you can experiment with the exercises to decide what's right for you. I am a firm believer in letting your own body tell you how much is too much or too little. As far as a guideline if you are unsure, I would start out doing two cable exercises for each body part if you are used to resistance training. If you haven't been training your muscles with heavy exercise, I would start out with one exercise for each body part and do two sets of each exercise.

Pick a resistance you can handle for about ten to twenty repetitions. With the positive movement of the exercise, as well as the negative, be sure not to jerk the cables or let the cables jerk you. Always keep constant pressure on the cables, and be sure with all cable exercises to keep a tight grip on the handles.

The main object, once again, is to start slowly, to get the feel of the cables. Once you are comfortable with the movements, you can advance to more sets and more exercises. As with weight training or any type of strength training, be sure to add resistance whenever possible, but don't be in too big a hurry to add more cables. You will progress at a consistent pace if you concentrate and train on a regular basis without missing workouts.

Now it's time to get started with the exercises. I also want to congratulate you, because you are about to enter a whole new world of training— a world where you can achieve a great deal of usable strength and flexibility, which can be carried over to your desired sport or activity.

So, good luck and good pulling!

Upper Body Exercises

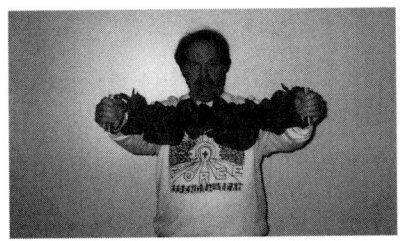 

3.1   Front Chest Pull

The front chest pull is one of the best chest and shoulder developers you can perform with cables. It is also one of the most well-known. To start, grasp the handles with your palms facing inward and start to pull outward and sideways, away from your body, until your arms form a cross, with your elbows locked and the cables stretched across your chest. Hold in this position for about a second, then return to the starting position, with your arms in front of you. Repeat the movement until fatigued.

Muscles worked: Chest, shoulders, upper back, traps.

 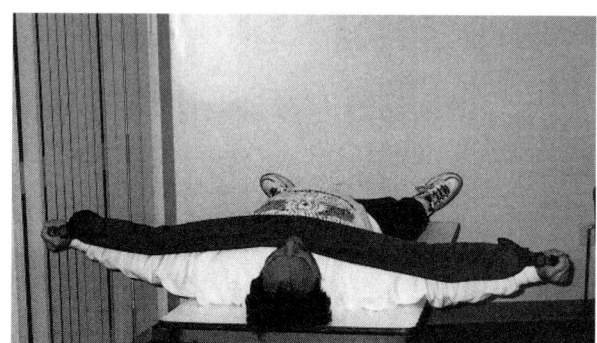

3.2   Bench Lateral Pull

This exercise is a great chest and shoulder developer, as well as a great exercise for flexibility. Lie flat on your back on a narrow bench. If you don't have a bench, you can position your upper body over the top of a footstool. Lie in a horizontal position holding the cables in front of you as though you were going to bench press them. Now pull the cables out sideways and downward so that the cables are stretching across your chest. Try to stretch your arms back past your chest to get the maximum benefit. However, do not stretch past your comfort zone. Repeat the exercise until fatigued.

Muscles worked: Chest, shoulders, traps.

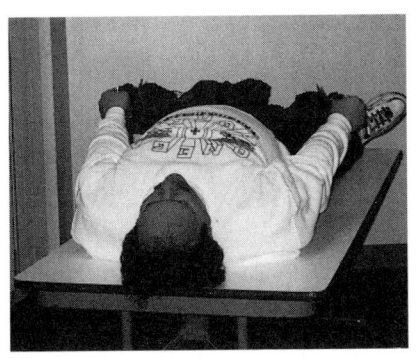 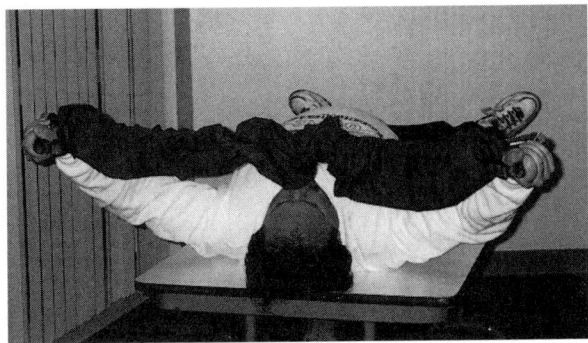

3.3 Cable Pullover

Here is a great chest and lung builder. If you concentrate on your breathing, you can also greatly expand your rib box, giving you a larger chest. Lie flat on your back on the floor or a bench, with your cables held across your thighs. Now slowly start to stretch your cables as you pull your arms straight over and behind your head. Hold this position for a couple of seconds and then return to the starting position. Repeat the process until fatigued.

Remember to breathe deeply on this exercise to get the best results. You can perform this exercise with your palms facing either inward or outward. I personally prefer the palms facing inward because it seems to be more comfortable on my wrists with this type of grip.

Muscles worked: Chest, shoulders, upper back.

3.4   Chest Forward Press

Place the cables around the middle of your back and pull them around and in front of you. Grasp the handles with your palms facing inward, and push or press the cables out in front of you until your arms are straight and your elbows are locked. Repeat the forward pressing movement until fatigued. This is a great chest developer and similar to a bench press except that you are in a standing position. If you are large-chested and not very flexible, you may have difficulty getting in the starting position. If this is so, start with light resistance at first. You will soon get a good feel for this exercise and gain flexibility in this position.

Muscles worked: Chest, shoulders, triceps.

3.5   Cable Crossover

This is a very good exercise for the chest. However, it is also very difficult at first. Start in the same position as the last exercise with your cables behind your back, at about the middle of your back. Pull the cables around and in front of you, and grasp them with your palms facing inward. From here, push the cables forward almost to the lockout position, then cross the cables over in front of you so that your arms are crossed in front of you. Tighten your chest muscles as you cross your arms. Note: Until you are used to this exercise, be careful not to cross your arms too far. Start by just crossing your arms slightly. Repeat the movement until tired.

Muscles worked: Chest, shoulders, triceps.

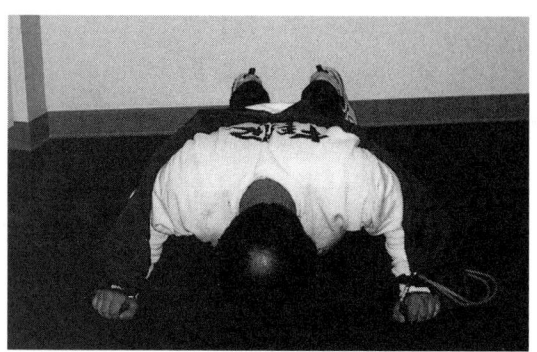 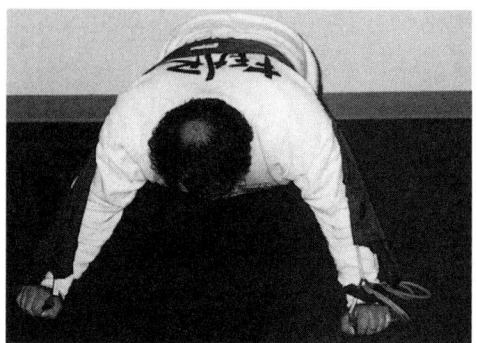

3.6   Cable Pushup

Our training would not be complete if cable pushups were not included. This exercise is a tremendous upper body developer. Start by placing the cables behind your back. They should be at the upper part of your back, but not too close to your neck, to keep them from slipping. Once they're behind your back and you're grasping the handles, get in a traditional pushup position in the down position. From here, with your hands securely over the top of the handles, press up into a pushup position, letting the cables supply resistance by stretching across your back. Continue with the pushups until fatigued. Of course, the more cables you use, the more resistance is placed upon you. This exercise alone is an absolute gold mine for gaining usable physical strength. As mentioned earlier, be sure to keep your hands securely over the top of the handles to prevent them from slipping.

Muscles worked: All pressing muscles of the upper body.

 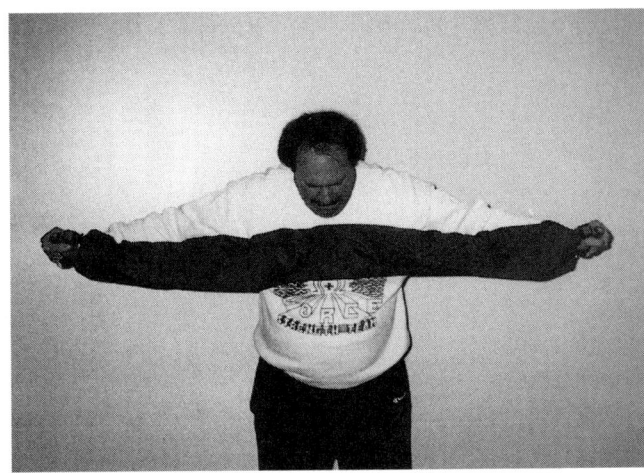

3.7   Front Lateral Raise

Here is a great shoulder developer you will want to include in your routine. Start with your arms down at your sides, holding the handles with your palms facing inward. From here stretch your cables as you pull your arms straight out to the sides at shoulder level, forming a cross. This is very similar to the crucifix lift with dumbbells. Be sure to use a good steady pull with this one to get the full benefits.

Muscles worked: Shoulders, upper back.

3.8   One-hand Lateral Raise

This exercise works the same muscles as the front lateral raise. I have
included this exercise because some people prefer to work one shoulder
at a time for better concentration. Start by putting your right foot well
inside one handle, securing it firmly on the floor. Now grasp the other
handle with your right hand and stretch the cables straight out to your
side in the lateral position. Repeat this movement on the right side until
fatigued, then work the left side. Be sure to keep a smooth and consistent pull on the cables throughout the entire movement.

Muscles worked: Shoulders, side angle.

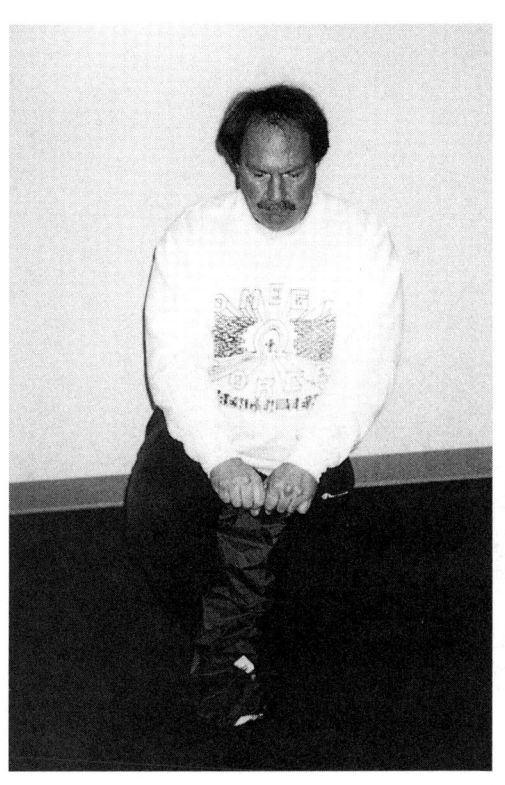 

3.9   Two-hands Frontal Raise

Here is another great shoulder exercise that works the shoulders from a different angle. Start by kneeling on your left leg, with your right leg bent at a ninety degree angle in front of you. Place your right foot well inside one handle and secure it firmly on the floor. Grasp the other handle with both hands, palms down, and with your arms straight, pull up the cables in front of you to shoulder height. Keep a steady pull throughout the movement. Repeat until fatigued. Be sure to keep your palms down on this movement.

Muscles worked: Front of shoulder, traps.

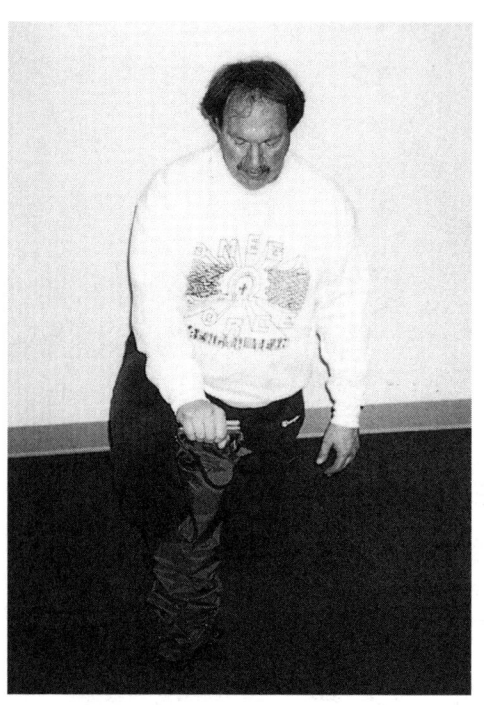 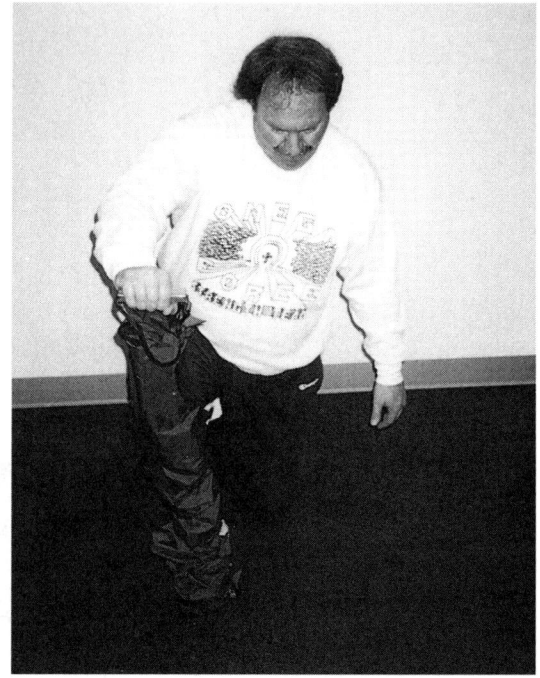

3.10 One-hand Frontal Raise

This exercise is just like the two-hands version except that one hand at a time is used instead of two. As I mentioned before, I included both versions because some prefer one style over the other. To start this exercise, kneel on your left leg, with your right leg bent at a ninety degree angle in front of you. Place your right foot well into the handle and secure it firmly on the floor. Grasp the other handle with your right hand, palm facing down and arm straight. Now raise your right arm straight up in front of you to shoulder level, keeping it straight throughout the entire movement. Be sure to keep a steady resistance at all times. Return to the starting position. Repeat the movement until fatigued, then work the left arm.

Muscles used: Front of shoulder, traps.

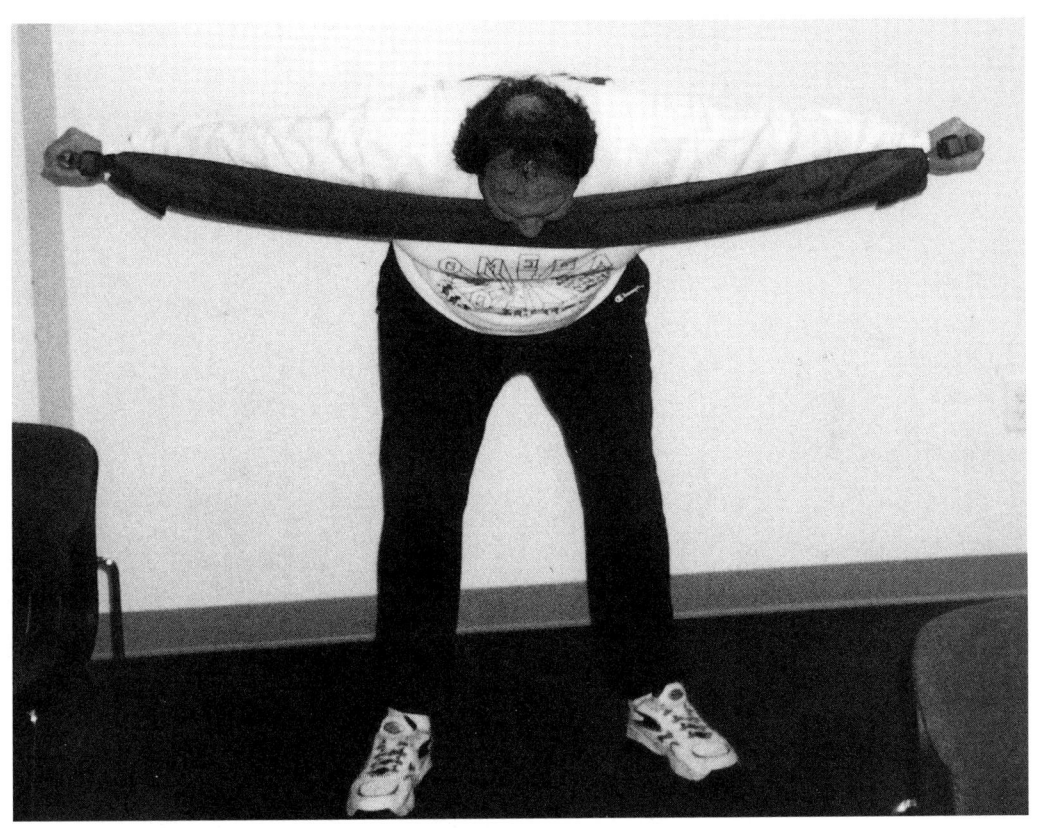

3.11   Bent Over Lateral Raise

This is a great rear shoulder builder that touches on the entire upper
body. Bend over at the waist and grasp the cables with your palms
facing inward. Start the exercise with your arms hanging down. Now
pull the cables out sideways and up until they touch your chest. Keep
your waist bent at all times and be sure to pull the cables out and
up as far as possible. Repeat until fatigued.

Muscles used: Shoulders, with emphasis on chest; upper back.

3.12   Back Lateral Raise

As you are probably starting to see by now, most cable exercises place stress on the shoulders. It is easy to see why the great cable pullers of the past had such great shoulder development, as well as great flexibility. This exercise is also excellent for shoulder development and flexibility. Start with the cables behind your back at upper thigh level. Grasp the handles with your palms facing upward and your arms straight. Now slowly pull the cables outward and upward to shoulder level. Be sure to keep a slow steady pressure throughout the movement. Return to the starting poistion, and repeat until fatigued.

Muscles worked: Shoulders, back, traps.

3.13 Overhead Downward Pull to Back

Here is a very popular exercise among the old-time cable pullers. It has great benefits, and it is easy to see why it was so popular. Start by holding the cables directly overhead with the palms facing inward. Now pull outward and downward slowly until the cables are stretched behind the back at shoulder level, forming a cross. Return to the original position above your head, and repeat the movement until fatigued. Be sure to keep a secure grip on the handles.

Muscles worked: Shoulders, back, triceps.

3.14   One-arm Press

This is another exercise which was popular among the old-time pullers. It is also a major pull in competition. Start by holding the cables diagonally across the back. Hold one handle down at your left side with a firm grip, palm facing downward. The right hand is grasping the other handle at shoulder level with your palm facing up. While holding your left hand down against your side with your arm straight, press your right arm directly overhead into the press position. Return the right arm back to shoulder level and repeat the movement until fatigued; then work the other side. Note: Be sure to keep other arm straight and against your side with a firm grip on the handle.

Muscles worked: Shoulders, triceps.

 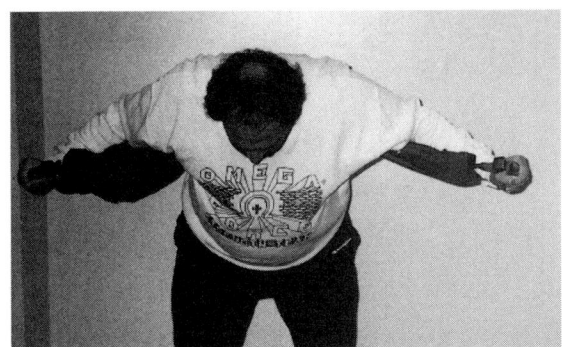

3.15   Bent Over Pressout

Here is an effective, but difficult exercise that will help develop your triceps to new levels. Bending at the waist, start by holding the cables behind your back at mid-back level, with your arms bent and your palms facing inward. Now slowly press the cables outward and to the sides as far as possible. Return slowly back to the starting position, and repeat the movement until fatigued. You may find it difficult to keep good control throughout the entire movement, so concentrate and you will soon master the control.

Muscles worked: Triceps, shoulders, upper back.

3.16   Overhead Downward Pull to Chest

Here is another great exercise for the shoulders and triceps. The starting
position is holding the cables directly overhead with the palms facing
inward. Now pull the cables outward and downward, until they are
stretched across your upper chest forming the cross position. Return
to the starting position, and repeat this exercise until fatigued.

Muscles worked: Shoulders, triceps.

3.17 Half Circle Back Raise

Here is another great exercise for the upper back and shoulders that will also greatly increase your flexibility. Start with the cables directly over your head with your palms facing outward. Now stretch the cables outward and downward until they are stretched behind your back at shoulder level, forming a cross. Be sure to keep a tight grip on the handles throughout the movement. Repeat until fatigued.

Muscles worked: Upper back, shoulders, triceps.

3.18   Back Pressout

This is perhaps the most popular exercise with the old-time cable pullers. It is one of the best exercises for building tremendous upper body strength. Start with your cables behind your mid-back, your hands grasping the handles with your palms facing inward. Now push outward, stretching the cables out until your arms are straight out at your sides, forming a cross. When returning to the starting position, be sure to resist the cables, keeping them from snapping. If you have a large upper body and are not very flexible, you may have difficulty with this one at first, but be patient and start with a light resistance, and you will soon reap great results from this great exercise.

Muscles worked: All pressing muscles of the upper body.

3.19 One-arm Pulldown

With this exercise, you can either perform it with your palms facing upward or downward. I prefer the palms facing downward because it seems to be more comfortable on the wrists. Start by grasping one handle with your left hand and holding it overhead, with your palm forward and your arm straight. The right hand is grasping the other handle palm downward, and the right arm is out in front of you, at about chest height. While keeping the left arm straight, pull the right arm sideways and downward to the thigh. Repeat the movement until fatigued; then work the other side.

Muscles worked: Chest, shoulders, upper back.

 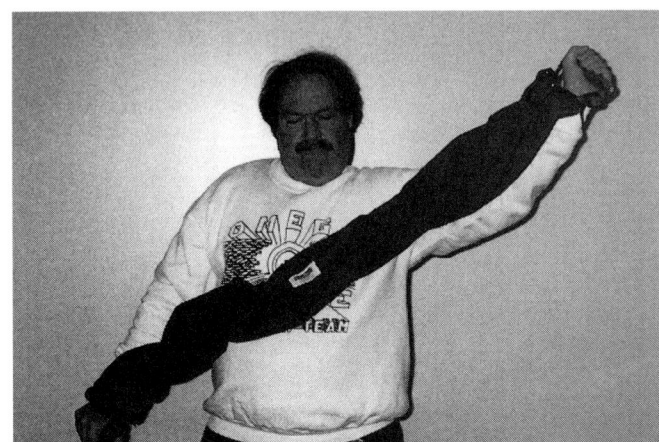

3.20   Chest Diagonal

This is a great exercise, but it is very difficult and demanding on the triceps muscles. Start with a light resistance to get used to the exercise. Begin by holding the cables diagonally in front of you, with the right arm at shoulder level, with the palm down. The left arm is fully bent at chest level, with the back of the hand facing upward. Now slowly stretch the cables, pulling the left arm down and out to your left side, and at the same time, pressing the right arm up and out to the right side, until both arms are straight. The cables are stretched diagonally across your chest. Return to the starting position, and repeat until fatigued, then switch positions and work the opposite side.

Muscles worked: Triceps, chest, shoulders.

3.21 Triceps Pressout

Here is a great triceps builder and one of my personal favorites. Start with the cables behind your neck, grasping the handles with your palms inward. Pull the cables outward forming a cross. Return to the original position and repeat the movement until fatigued. Really try to concentrate on this one throughout the movement. You will experience a tremendous pump in your triceps as a result of this exercise. I can also say from experience that if you work on this exercise consistently and progressively, you will experience continued growth in your arm size, due to the triceps muscle development. Be sure to keep a tight grip on the handles throughout the movement.

Muscles used: Triceps, shoulders, upper back.

3.22   Triceps Extension

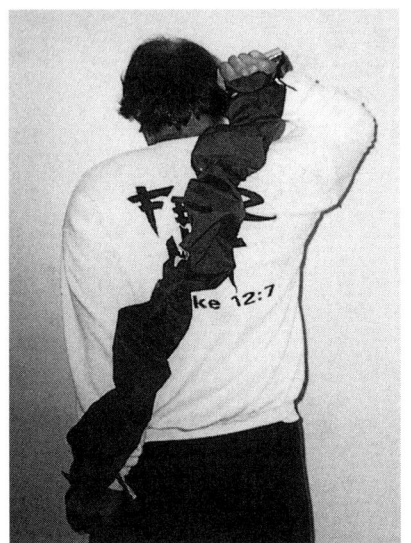

Here is another great triceps builder.
Start with the cables behind your back,
holding one end of the cables down at
your left side with the left arm straight,
palm down. The right arm is bent at
shoulder height, with the right hand
grasping the other handle, palm upward,
by your right ear. While keeping your left
arm straight down at your side, extend
the right arm, which is at the right side
of your head, straight up into a press or
lockout position. Return the right arm
to the side of the head, and repeat the
movement until fatigued. Switch sides
to develop both arms evenly.

Muscles worked: Triceps, shoulders.

 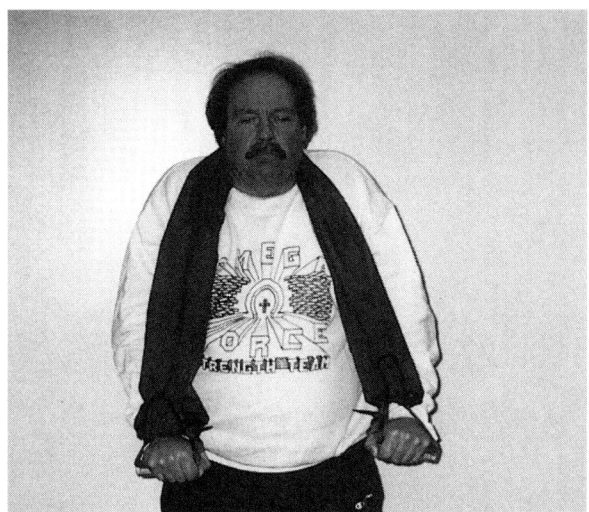

3.23 Triceps Pressdown

Here is a favorite triceps builder usually practiced with weights, only we are going to perform it with cables instead. I think you will find that the resistance of cables on this exercise is a steadier pull. You will also experience a stronger resistance in the negative pull with cables. Start by placing the cables around the back of your neck, with the handles hanging in front of you at your upper chest. Grasp a handle with each hand, palms down, and straighten your arms against the resistance of the cables. Be sure to press the cables straight down as in a traditional triceps pressdown. You may wish to use a towel behind your neck to prevent the cables from rubbing. Return your arms to the original position and repeat until fatigued. Be sure to resist the pressure on the negative part of the movement.

Muscles worked: Triceps.

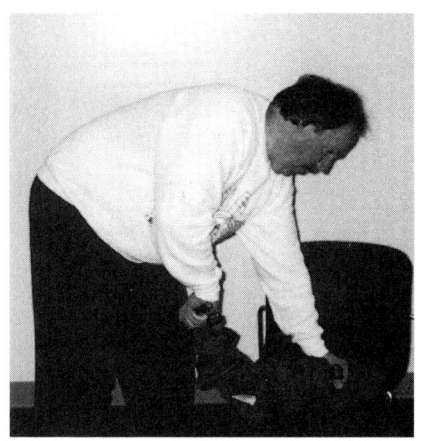 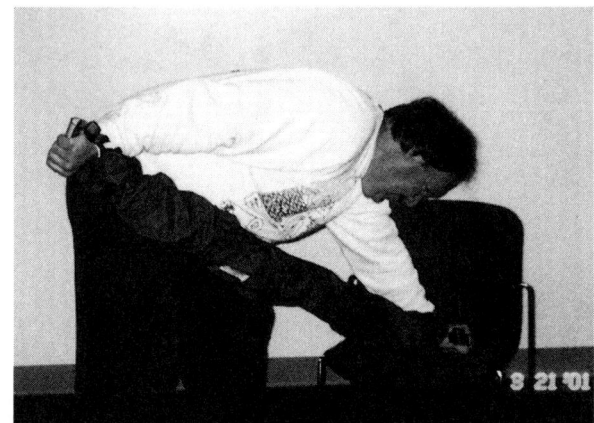

3.24   Triceps Kickback

This exercise is great for isolating the triceps muscle. Bend over slightly at the waist to start the exercise. Grasp one handle in your right hand and place it firmly on a bench or chair, keeping your arm straight. Grasp the other handle in your left hand. Your palm can be facing either up or down on this exercise; either way will work the triceps, but at just a little different angle. Your left arm should be hanging straight down toward the ground. Now extend your left arm straight back and up against the resistance of the cables. Return to the starting position and repeat until fatigued; then work the right arm. Be sure to keep steady pressure on the cables throughout this movement and concentrate on the triceps.

Muscles worked: Triceps, rear of shoulder.

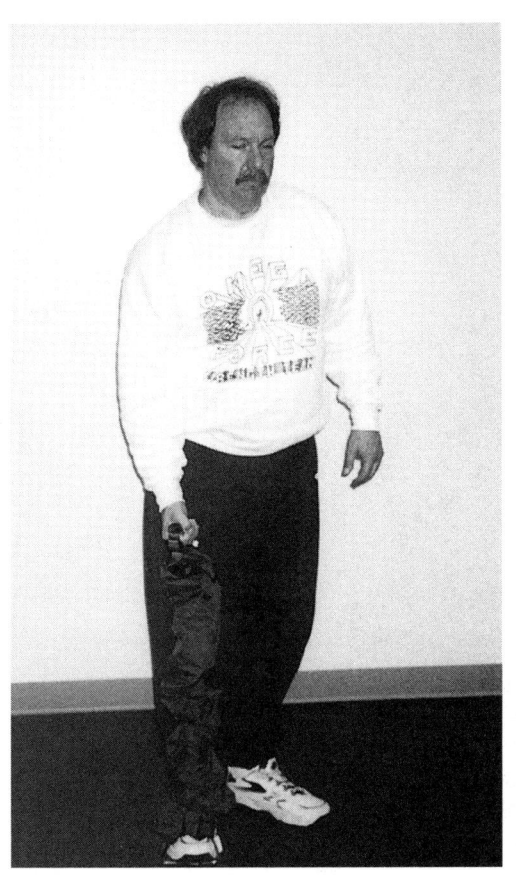 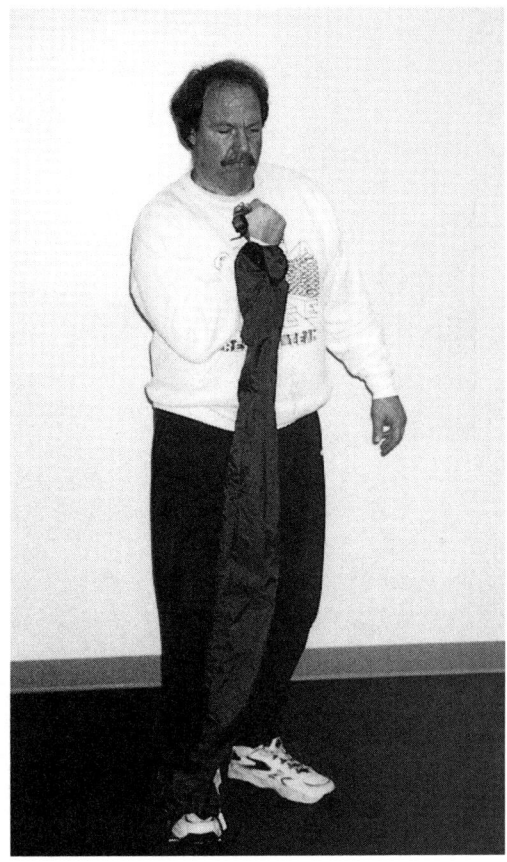

3.25   Biceps Curl

With cables you will be surprised how good a pump you can obtain with the standard biceps curl. Start by firmly standing on one handle of the cables with your right foot, securing it to the floor, and placing the other handle in your right hand, palm up. Start with your arm straight and curl the cables up to your shoulder, keeping a steady pull on the cables throughout the movement. Return your right hand to the starting position and repeat the movement until fatigued; then work the left arm.

Muscles worked: Biceps, forearms.

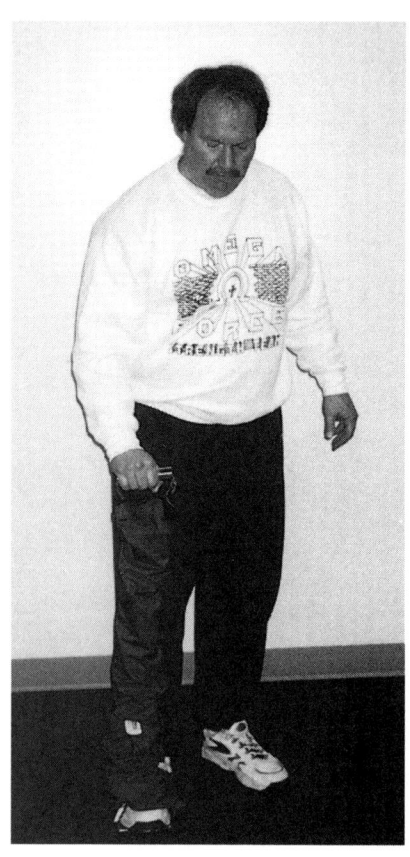 

3.26   Reverse Curl

The reverse curl is another popular form of the curl which is done with cables. Start by standing on one handle with your right foot, securing it firmly to the floor. Grasp the other handle with your right hand, with your palm down and your arm straight down. Now curl the cables up to your shoulder with a slow, steady pull. Return the right hand to the starting position and repeat the movement until fatigued; then change hands and work the left arm. Keep a tight grip on the handles throughout the movement.

Muscles worked: Biceps, forearms

Exercises with Shortened Cables

In Questions and Answers (Chapter 4), we will discuss the importance of shortening the cables on certain exercises to get a full range of motion. To shorten your cables, remove them from your set and double them up, looping them around twice. This cuts the length in half and makes them twice as strong or resistant. Now all you have to do is place the doubled cables back on the set, and you are ready to perform exercises that were difficult to do before with the longer cables and greater range of motion.

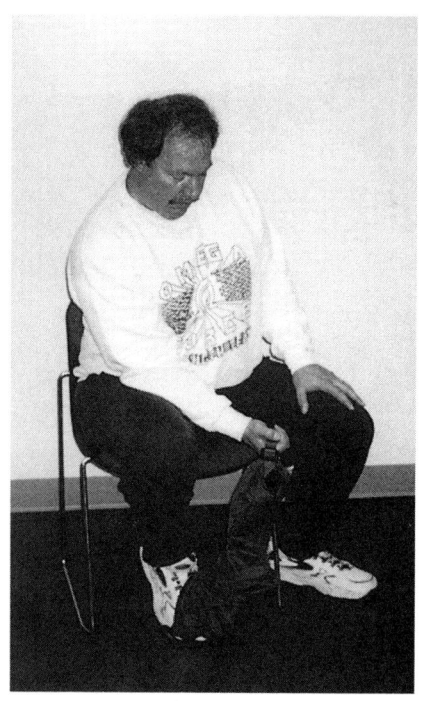 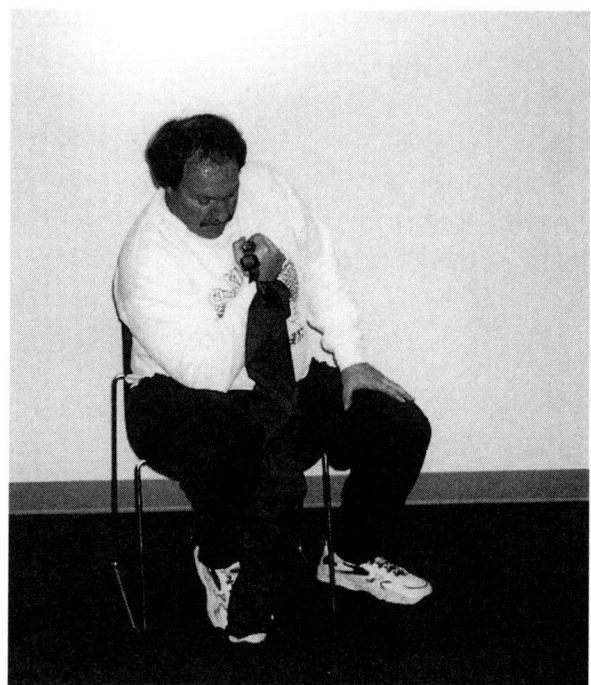

3.27   Concentration Curl

The seated concentration curl is a prime example of an exercise that requires shortened cables. To perform, sit in a chair or on a bench, and place your right foot well through and on top of one of the handles, pinning it securely to the floor. Grasp the other handle with your right hand. Your right arm should be against the inside of your thigh. Curl the cables up to your chest with a steady motion. Return to the starting position and repeat the movement; then work the left arm. Note that with the cables doubled, you will feel a tremendous resistance on the negative movement.

Muscles worked: Biceps, forearms.

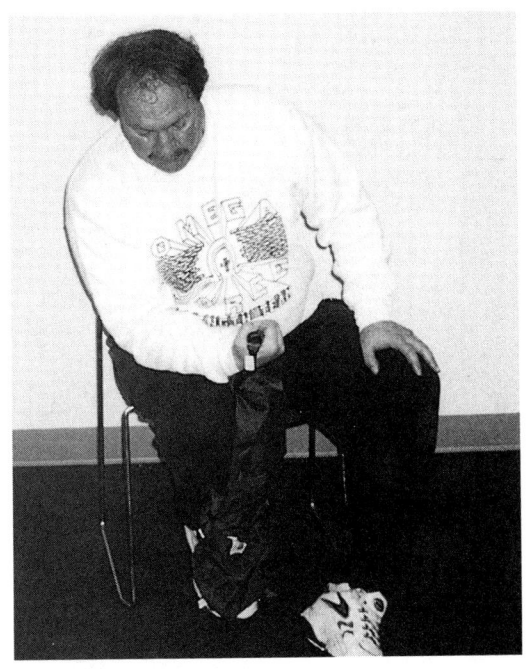

3.28   Short Cable Wrist Curl

Here is another great exercise requiring shortened cables. The classic wrist curl is important for anyone embarking on any kind of strength training program. Start by sitting in a chair or on the end of a bench. Place your right foot well into one of the handles, pinning it securely to the floor.

Grasp the other handle with your right hand, stretching the cables so that you can place your right forearm on your thigh, with your wrist and hand hanging over the side. Now simply bend your wrist up and down against the resistance of the cables. Repeat until fatigued, and then switch to the other hand for equal development. Oftentimes when working your forearms with wrist curls, you may want to do a higher number of repetitions than you would with other exercises.

Muscles worked: Wrists, forearms.

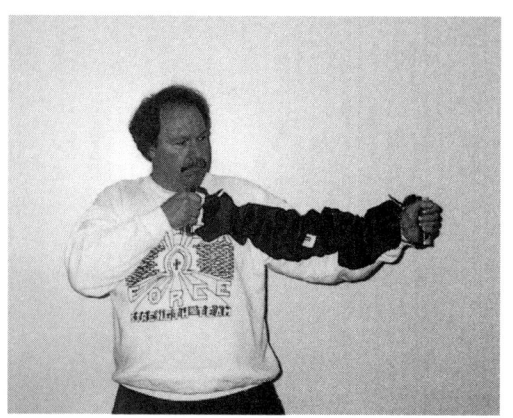

3.29   Archer with Short Cables

The archer, or the bow and arrow pull, is a very popular cable exercise. In fact, it may be the most popular pull, next to the front chest pull, that there is. It is another exercise which requires shortened cables. To start, grasp a cable handle in each hand. One hand is pulling and the other hand is pushing, just like drawing a bow. Extend one arm straight and hold it straight throughout the movement. The other arm pulls back the cables as far as possible. Return to the original position and repeat the movement until fatigued; then work the other side.

Muscles worked: Entire upper body.

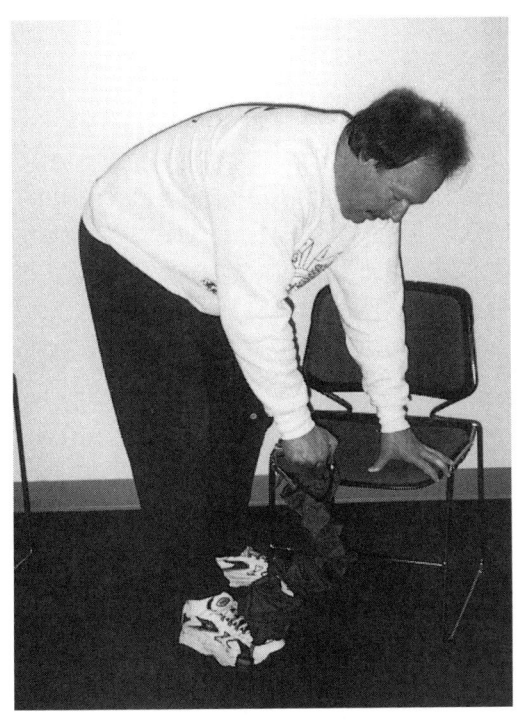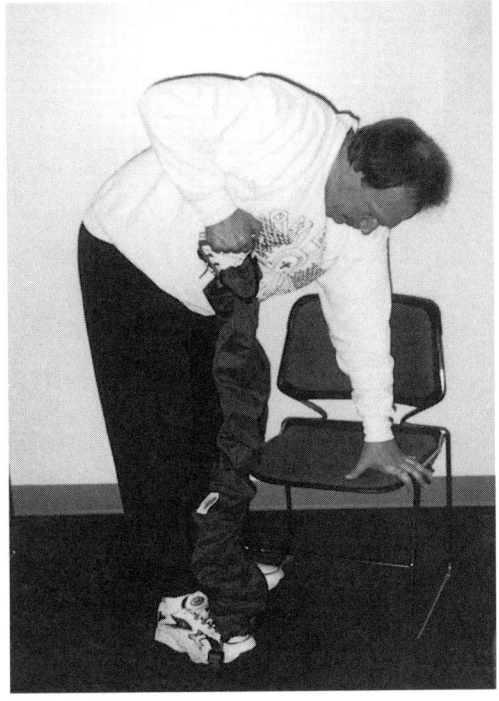

3.30   One-arm Row with Short Cables

Here is a great exercise for developing the lat muscles. Once again, this exercise is done with shortened cables. Start by leaning over a bench or chair. It is best to use a bench so that you can place your knee on the bench, but if you don't have one, you can use a chair. Once in this position, place your right foot securely through one handle of the cables, securing it firmly on the floor, and grasp the other handle in your right hand. Now pull the cables up to your chest in a rowing type fashion. Bring your arm back to the original position and repeat the movement until fatigued; then work the other arm.

Muscles worked: Lats, biceps, forearms.

have mentioned a few exercises which require shortened cables. However, there are others you may find useful with shortened cables as well, like the one-hand deadlift. It is amazing how much resistance there is on a few cables that have been doubled and shortened, when they are stretched out. Always be aware of the powerful negative pressure that is on the cables in any exercise, particularly the ones done with shortened cables. As I have mentioned before, cables work your muscles differently from any other type of training.

Exercises with Cable Attachments

A variety of handles or accessories can be attached to your cable set so you can train with a different angle or grip. I have many different types of homemade attachments which aid in certain exercises. We will discuss two attachments you can easily add that can be a huge help to you in your training. We will also mention a few different exercises that can be done with these attachments.

First of all, let's look at the ordinary towel. Yes, the towel is a great asset to some cable training exercises. You should use a towel that is strong and free of tears for the sake of safety. Once you have chosen a towel, put the towel through one handle so that the two ends of the towel can be grasped by your hand.

You are now ready to do a variety of exercises. These exercises can also be done with both hands at the same time, instead of one hand at a time. By using the towel, you will develop and work your grip to the extreme. I would suggest adding a couple of towel exercises to your training.

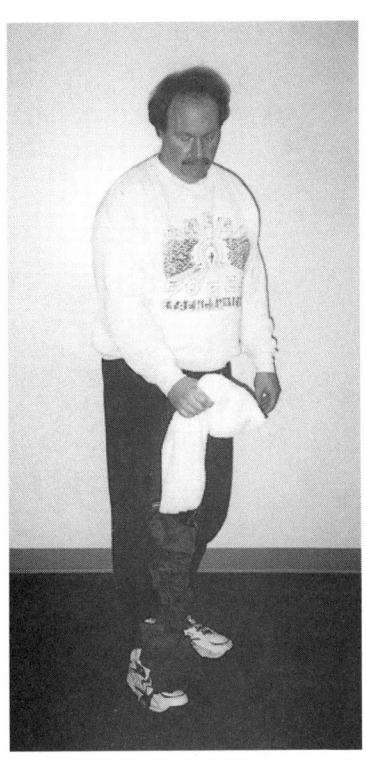 

3.31 Hammer Curl with Towel

Here is an excellent exercise for anyone, but if you are an arm wrestler, you will definitely want to do this one. Start by placing your right foot well through one handle and pinning it securely to the floor. Put the towel through the other handle, and grasp both ends of the towel with the right hand. Keeping your back straight, hammer curl the cables up to your upper chest while holding onto the towel. Lower to the starting position while keeping the movement steady, and repeat movement until fatigued. Then change arms and work the other side. You may need to use shortened cables to get a full range of motion.

Muscles used: Shoulders, biceps, forearms.

Other great exercises that can be performed with the towel attachment are different types of rowing exercises. Let's look at seated rowing.

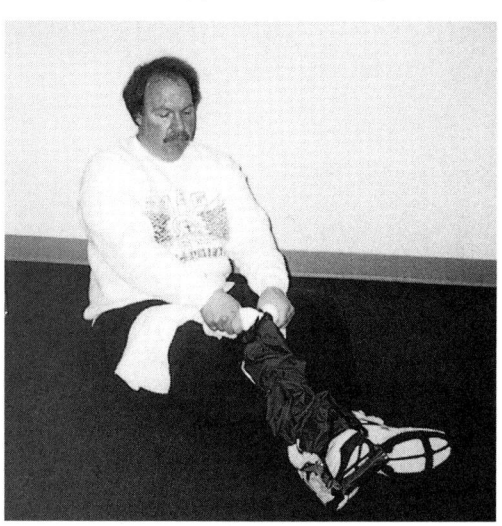 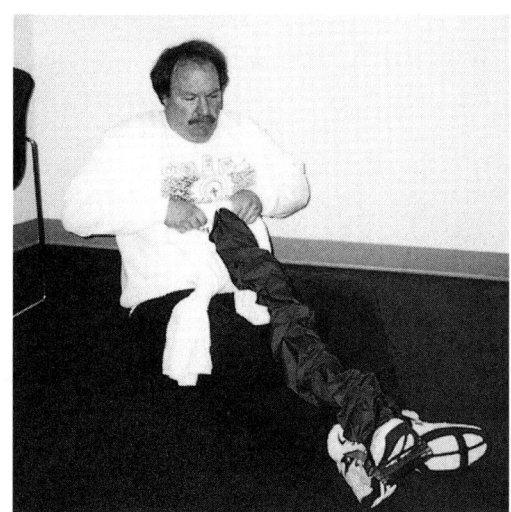

3.32   Seated Row with Towel

To perform this exercise, you may need to shorten the cables to get a better range of motion. Start by sitting on the floor, with one foot placed securely through one of the handles. Putting the towel through the other handle, hold onto the ends of the towel with both hands. While keeping your legs straight, pull back on the towel, stretching the cables. Return to the starting position and repeat the movement. Be sure to keep your legs straight, and be sure your foot is securely through the handle. Concentrate on using your lats for the main pulling force.

Muscles worked: Upper back muscles.

3.33
Triceps Extension with Towel

Here is a great exercise for the triceps. You will want to use the cables at regular length for this one. Start by placing one foot well through one of the handles, securing it firmly on the floor. Now pull the cables up through your legs and behind your back. Putting the towel through the other handle, grasp the ends of the towel with your hands and press them overhead,

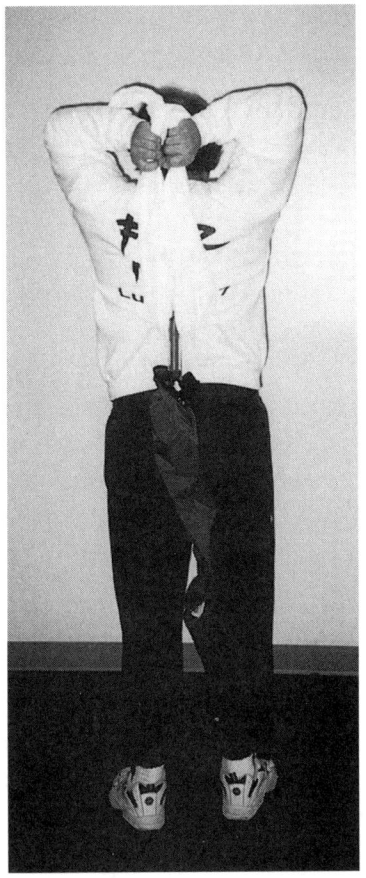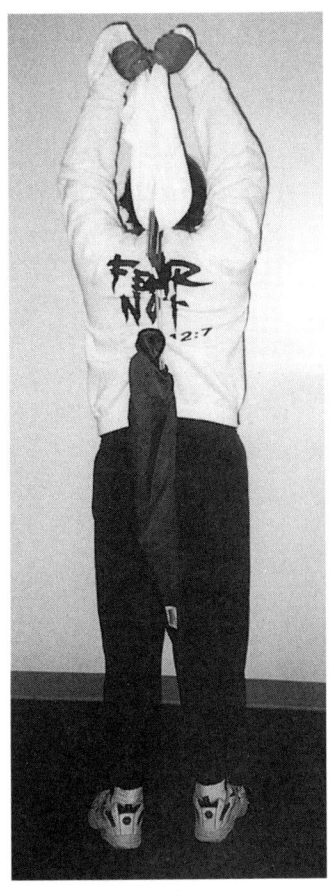

using only your triceps. Return to the starting position and repeat the movement. An important note: You will need to use a light resistance on this exercise due to the distance that the cables are being stretched. You will find it difficult to get the cables in the right position if you use too much resistance. On this movement, the cables will be stretched far enough to supply you with all the resistance you need.

Muscles used: Triceps, shoulders.

As I mentioned earlier there are many, many exercises that are great with the towel attached. We have touched on just a few, but with a little innovative thinking, the sky's the limit.

I would also like to mention again that the towel exercises give your hand and wrist muscles a great workout. If you are interested in developing your grip to great extremes, you can perform some towel exercises with one hand instead of two hands. For instance, seated rowing or triceps extensions could be done by grasping both ends of the towel with just one hand instead of two hands. You will be surprised how well performing these towel exercises with one hand works the hand muscles. You are also making the gripped object, which is the towel, twice as thick, placing greater stress on the fingers. Be careful to keep a secure grip on the towel at all times.

The other attachment that we will discuss is a pole or a bar. Yes, by using a simple bar, you can have access to a whole world of exercises. As far as choosing a bar for your exercises, you can use a heavy mop handle, a sturdy dowel rod, or even a steel bar or rod—anything that is strong enough to support the resistance of the cables. Once you have chosen a bar, you can get started on the exercises.

I don't think it's necessary to go through a whole lot of exercises to show you how to use the bar attachment. For example, you can do curls by standing on one of the cables with your foot through and on top of the handle, held securely to the floor. With the bar placed through the other handle, grasp the bar in the same way you would grasp a barbell. Now you can do a set of curls in traditional fashion. Wrist curls are performed by firmly holding one cable handle down on the foor with your foot in the same fashion as the curls. You then place the bar through the other handle, grasp the bar with palms up, place your wrists over your knees and perform classic wrist curls. Reverse curls and reverse wrist curls are performed the same way, except your hands are turned over, palms facing down toward the floor. As you can see, the possibilities with cables are almost endless.

There are many, many other exercises performed with a bar attachment. Just to mention a few, you can perform all types of rowing movements, deadlifts, and even overhead presses. As with any exercise program, you have to find the methods and movements that work best for you. They are all good exercises, but some, of course, will meet your needs better than others. One goal I had with these exercises was to give you a variety to choose from.

Leg Exercises

Here are some actual leg training exercises performed with cables. I know many of you are saying that you thought cables are only used to train your upper body. Well, for the most part, cables are made for upper body training. I certainly feel that cables are a much better upper body training tool than lower body. They are more practical and convenient for the upper body as well. However, with a little innovation, you can find many exercises to train your legs—exercises that actually work.

While training with cables of different kinds through the years, I have found many exercises to build great leg strength and flexibility. I feel this course would be incomplete if I didn't show you some of the exercises I have found. I'm not going to include all of the exercises you can perform, as there are too many and some require a little different set-up that would be hard to explain, but I think the ones included will give you a good taste of just how practical cables are.

3.34   Front Squat with Bar

Here is a classic thigh developer. The front squat is one of the best leg
training exercises and can be performed with cables. All you need is a
bar attachment like the one we talked about in the preceding section on
using cables with attachments. Place one of your feet well through one
handle and securely pin it to the floor. Place the bar through the other
handle, and you are ready to begin. Squat down in the bottom position
and place the bar under the front of your neck and against your

shoulders. Hold the bar with your hands and stand straight up against the resistance of the cables. Return to the squat position and repeat until fatigued. Be sure to keep the bar attachment against your body during the entire movement. This exercise will give you a great pump in the front of your thighs.

Muscles worked: Entire hip area and legs.

You may wish to perform this exercise with one leg instead of two, to enhance your balance as well as your strength. You will also learn that by doing one-legged squats over two-legged, you will develop strength that can be used in sports. This is not to say that regular squats aren't productive, because we all know they are; but I guarantee you, if you start a program of one-legged squats, you will notice a great difference in your balance and leg strength when you play any type of sport, whether competitive or leisure.

To perform this exercise, set up in the same manner as the front squat, but squat off one leg instead of two legs. Start slowly with this exercise; you may find it more difficult than you think. It places a lot of stress on your thighs, and you may have difficulty balancing at first. Your ultimate goal is to be able to balance and squat on that one leg, but at first, to get started, use a box or short chair or anything that will help you balance. Once you are balanced, start to squat up and down on that leg until you are fatigued. Be sure to rotate to the other leg to exercise both legs equally.

3.35   One-legged Squat Holding Handle

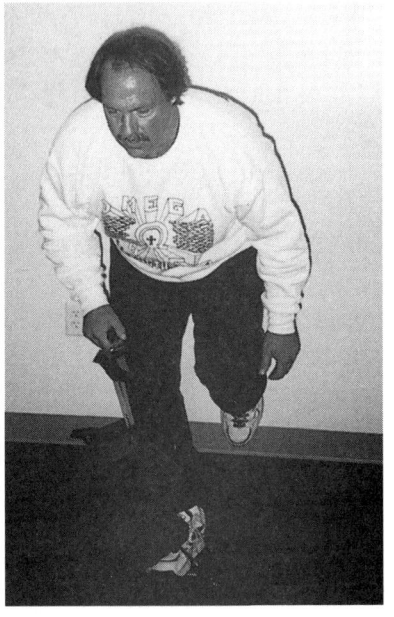

Here is another version of the one-legged squat. Place your right foot well through and securely on top of one of the handles, pinning it to the floor, and grasp the other handle with your right hand. Your left leg is held off the floor, behind you. Now squat down into the bottom position and, while holding the handle securely, stand back up, straightening your right leg. Return to the squatting position and repeat the movement until fatigued; then work your left side. You may also want to use a box to help you balance; however, it is impor-tant to progress to the point where you can perform the one-legged squat without any aid.

Muscles worked: Entire hip area and legs.

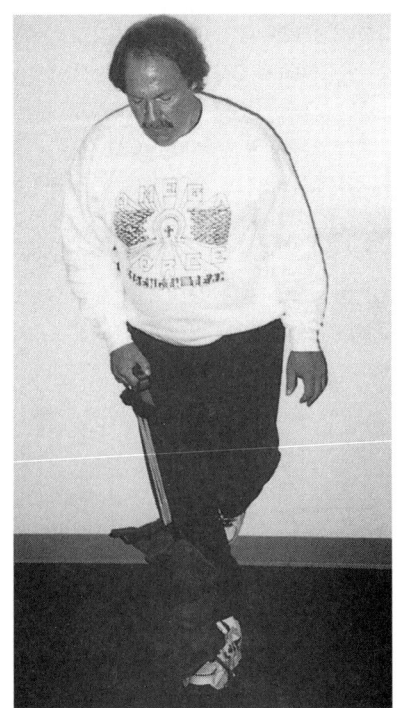

I would strongly suggest that you try a one-legged squat program whether you are interested in developing great strength, or improving your performance in sports. I will conclude by saying that the one-legged squat is worth its weight in gold.

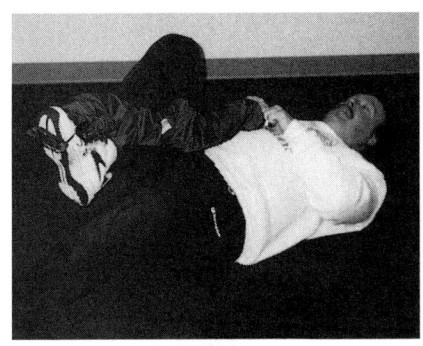 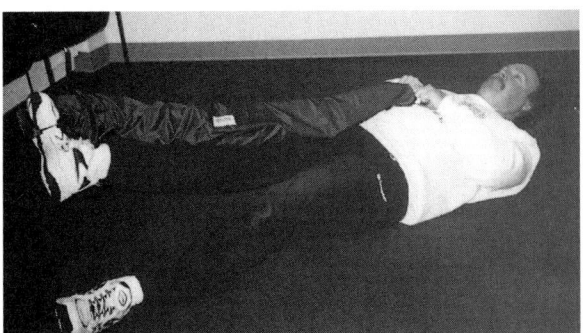

3.36 Lying One-legged Press

Here is a beauty of an exercise that must be tried to be appreciated. To look at it, it doesn't appear to be too difficult. You may want to shorten the cables to get the full effect. Start by placing one foot well and securely through one handle. Lie on your back with your arms straight on top of your body, holding the other handle of the cable set. While keeping your arms straight and grasping the handle with both hands (you may wish to use a bar attachment for a better grip), bring your foot with the handle secured back toward your face slightly. Now press with your foot against the resistance until your leg is straight. Return to the original position and repeat the movement until fatigued. Be sure to work both legs equally. Be careful on this exercise, making sure to secure a safe foothold in the cable handle. You will be surprised how much pressure there is on the shortened cables when they are fully stretched.

Muscles worked: Entire hip area and legs.

3.37 Standing Leg Press

Here is another exercise that is deceptively difficult. Like the last exercise, there is more to it than meets the eye. The standing leg press is not only a good strength builder, but also an excellent exercise for developing a great sense of balance. I can't stress enough that many of these cable exercises are truly a gold mine for athletic performance.

For this exercise, start by placing one foot well into one of the handles, making sure it is securely in place. Bring your knee up, holding the other handle with both hands at chest height. Now straighten your leg, pressing the handle to the floor, against the resistance of the cables. Slowly return your foot to the starting position, resisting the pressure of the cables throughout the movement. You can also use a bar attachment through the handle, holding the bar against your upper chest as though you were performing a front squat, or as though you had just cleaned the bar to your shoulders.

You can get a really good range of motion with this exercise, so concentrate and put a lot into it. Be sure to perform the same number of sets on each leg. You may also want to do quite a few repetitions on this exercise to build great leg endurance.

Muscles worked: Entire hip area and legs.

3.38   Outward Stretch

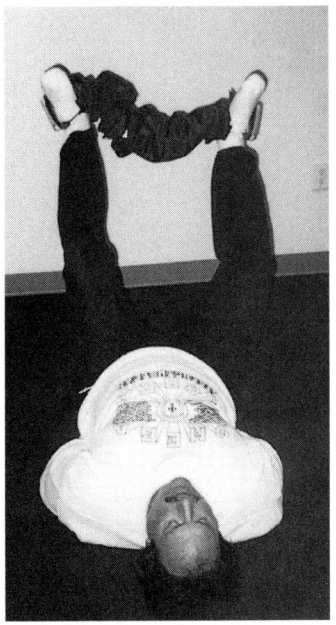

Here is a great exercise for the hips and the outer thighs. It is not only a strength builder, but also a great way to gain flexibility in your hips. This exercise is a must for wrestlers and swimmers. Start by lying on the floor with your feet through each of the cable handles. Be sure that your feet are very secure in the handles. Lie back on the floor and start to pull your legs apart against the resistance of the cables. Stretch the cables as far as possible without straining. Return slowly to the starting position and repeat the exercise until fatigued. Be sure to keep a steady amount of pressure against the cables throughout the entire movement. This is also a good exercise to help prevent injury in athletics, because of the increased flexibility you will develop after performing this movement for a while. Be sure to have a very secure foothold on the handles while performing this exercise.

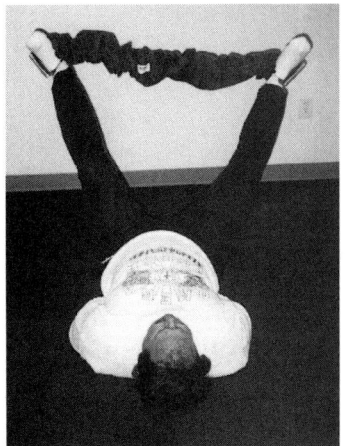

Muscles worked: Hips and outer thighs.

3.39 Calf Extension

Believe it or not, you can even work your calves with cables. While playing around one day, I found a way to get a great pump in my lower legs. At one time I was doing traditional calf raises with cables, but I was always at risk of the cables slipping out from under my heels when I raised them up, so instead I do calf extensions. Start by sitting in a chair or on the side of a bench. Grasp one handle with both hands and place your foot firmly and securely into the other handle. Straighten your leg to tighten the tension on the cables. Once you have enough tension on the cables, begin to work your foot back and forth against the tension. Use as much range of motion as possible to get the full effect. If you concentrate, you will be surprised at how effective this exercise can be. It is basically like doing toe raises in the traditional fashion, except you don't have the weight on your shoulders. Be sure to keep a secure foothold throughout the movement; work both legs equally.

Muscles worked: Calves.

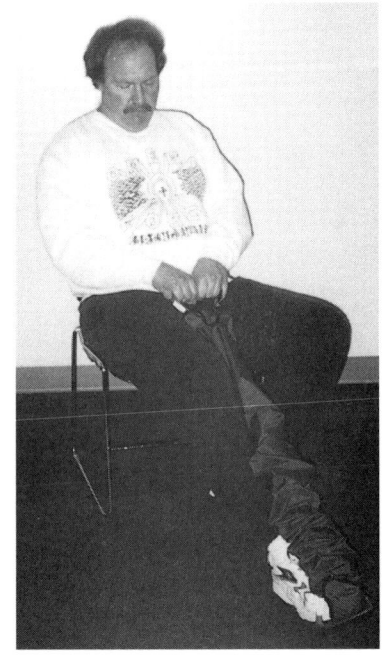

3.40 Front Calf Extension

Here is another lower leg exercise, only this time we're going to work the front of the lower leg instead of the back. You rarely see or hear of anyone working the front of the lower leg, but to achieve complete lower leg development, you need to include an exercise for the front of the lower leg as well. Start by shortening the cables. Sit on the end of a bench or in a chair. Now place one foot firmly and securely in each handle, with one leg straight and the other leg bent at the knee. Keeping one leg straight, pull back against the tension of the cables by extending your foot back and forth. This movement can really give you a great burn in the front of your lower leg. Be sure to train both legs equally.

Muscles worked:
Fronts of lower legs.

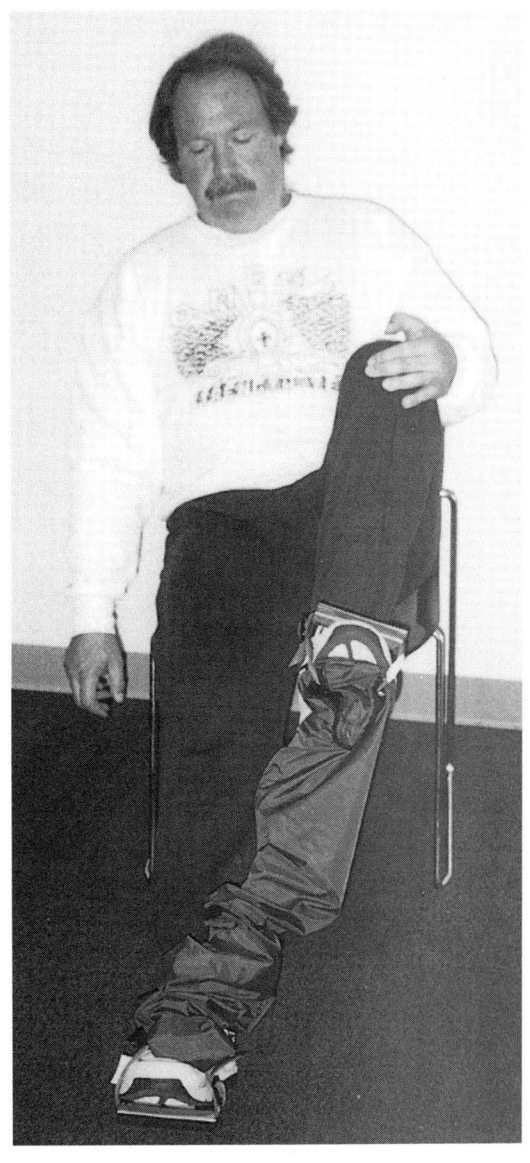

have given you a handful of exercises for your legs that can be per-formed practically with cables and with results. As I mentioned before, there are many more applications you can use for your legs that aren't mentioned. I would suggest trying some of these leg exercises if you are involved in sports. They will increase your balance and flexibility by leaps and bounds, making you a force to be reckoned with in your chosen field. Always remember that cross-training with exercises will help you climb to new heights.

Stretches with Cables

We have talked earlier about how important flexibility is in the upper body. It protects you from injury, increases your longevity, and builds your strength in many movements, due to a better range of motion in the upper body, especially in the shoulders. When this takes place, you are able to use your full strength in positions and at angles that before were disadvantageous due to a lack of flexibility. In this section we will look at some cable exercises that are designed to increase your flexibility and your range of motion, thus improving your strength in the process. It is also a good idea to include a couple of these in your routine as a warmup at the start of your workout.

I would also like to make the point that if you have been pulling cables for a while and have found it difficult to jump up in resistance on certain exercises, you may want to include a couple of these stretches in your routine. I can almost guarantee you that your strength will improve on those difficult exercises as a result. There are many variations of these stretches, and I have included several basic ones to get you started. Even though they are basic, they will give you a great advantage in your sport, activity, or strength goals. Try them out and see which ones work best for you.

 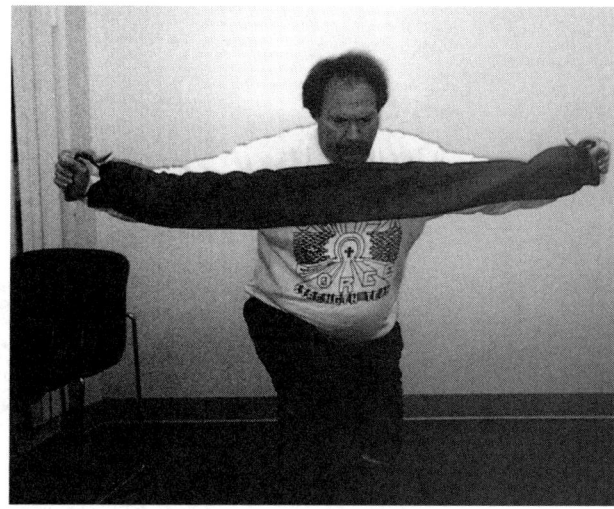

3.41   Body Lunge

Here is a great stretch to start each workout. It will loosen up the shoulders and chest, as well as get the circulation going throughout your entire body.

Start by standing at attention holding the cables in front of your chest. Your palms can be facing inward or outward. Now lunge forward with one leg and at the same time lift your arms upwards and out to the sides until you get a good stretch in your upper body. Try to gradually increase your range of motion on this exercise without forcing it. Return to the starting position, and continue to repeat the exercise until you feel loosened up. Also be sure to do the lunges alternating each leg.

Muscles stretched: Entire body, with emphasis on the shoulders.

3.42   Shoulder Rotation

Here is a world-class exercise for developing great flexibility in the shoulders. Be sure to start with light resistance on this exercise until you get used to it. Also remember that with all these stretches, the object is not to see how much resistance you can use, but to loosen up and gain flexibility in your shoulders so that you can achieve your athletic goals and be less prone to injury.

Start this exercise by holding the cables behind your back at your upper thigh with your palms facing inward. Now lift the arms straight up and over your head and then down to the front of your thighs. Return to the original position and repeat the movement until you're well stretched in the shoulders. Really concentrate on this one, and it will do wonders for you.

Muscles stretched: Shoulders.

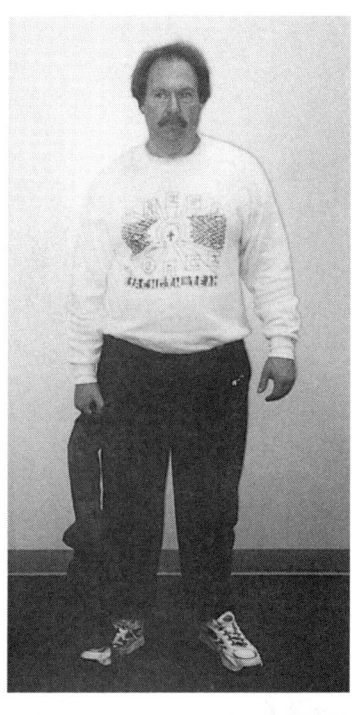

3.43   Side Bend

Here is a great stretch for your entire body. It is a traditional stretch, but it becomes much more productive when cables are added. Start by placing your right foot well through one handle and pinning it firmly to the floor. Grasp the other handle with your right hand, palm facing inward. Bend over to your left side, reaching your left arm down toward the floor and pulling up with your right arm on the cables. Return to the original position and repeat the movement until stretched.   Be sure to stretch both sides equally, and also use a slow, steady stretch throughout the movement.

Muscles used: Entire body is stretched.

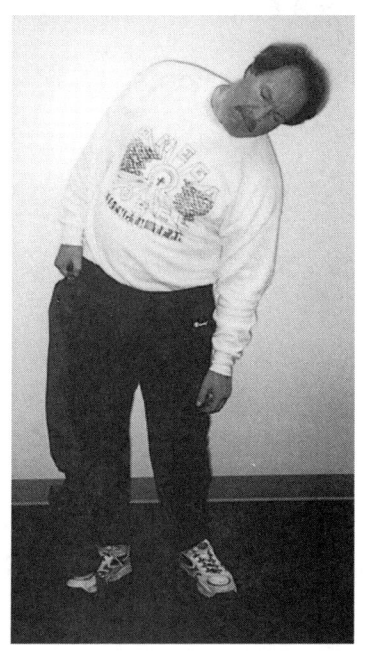

3.44   Abdominal Stretch

Here is a great stretch that brings the whole body into play. It is also a great exercise for building flexibility and coordination. Start by sitting on the side of a bench or sturdy stool. Be sure to anchor your feet under a strong piece of furniture or weight. Hold the cables in front of your body with your palms facing inward. Now pull the cables out across your chest as far as you can while you are lowering your upper body backward toward the floor. You are basically doing a traditional Roman chair situp in unison with the cable stretch.

Lean back as far as you can without straining. Return to the starting position, letting the cables return to their original position as well. Continue this exercise until fatigued.

Muscles used: Abdominals, upper body.

3.45   Cable Knee Bend

Here is another exercise that will help you develop good coordination and balance. Concentrate on the balance aspect, for it is not as easy as it appears. Start by standing with the cables straight above your head with your palms inward. Now pull the cables downward and outward across your back as far as you can at the same time as you perform a knee bend or squat. Hold in the squat position for a second or two, then return to the original standing position, bringing the cables overhead again. Repeat the movement until fatigued.

Muscles used: Entire body.

These are just a few exercises designed to increase your flexibility, balance, and coordination. Once again, I suggest that you add a couple of these to your routine to make you more flexible and durable. I noticed a huge difference in my strength levels in certain positions after adding some stretching exercises with the cables. So, try some stretches and stretch your performance to new levels.

Cables for Arm Wrestling

Cables can be an especially productive tool of trade for the arm wrestler. Whether you use the hook, the shoulder roll, or the top roll, you can profit from cable pulling. Of course, the regular cable exercises will enhance your strength at the arm wrestling table. Also, there are ways to simulate actual pulling techniques with the cables. Let's look at how you can simulate some pulls.

3.46   The Hook with Cables

The hook was the most popular style of arm wrestling years ago. It is still practiced by some professionals, but is becoming a little outdated next to the top roll. Of course, the average leisure arm wrestler still relies on it.

To simulate the hook with cables, attach your cables to one of the bars on a weight bench. If you cannot loop your handle over the bar, tie a towel or a rope around the bar and through the cable handle. You may also wish to shorten your cables for more resistance. Once you have one end of the cables hooked to the bench, grasp the other handle, with your elbow on the bench. Now you are ready to pull against the cables, as though you were pulling against an opponent. If you don't have a bench, you can attach one end of the cables to the leg of a heavy piece of furniture and place your elbow on a stool or the seat of a chair.

3.47   The Top Roll with Cables

The top roll is now one of the most popular techniques among professional arm wrestlers. Here is a way to develop almost limitless strength
in pulling-back pressure. Start by hooking your cables to the bar of a
bench, or the leg of a heavy piece of furniture as in the last exercise.
Your elbow, once again, is placed on a bench or stool. This time, put a
towel through the handle you are pulling; place the two ends together
and grasp them with your hand. Now you are ready to pull the cables
straight back the same way you would apply back pressure against an
opponent.

With both of these exercises, be sure to add resistance whenever possible. You will learn to love these exercises if you are an arm wrestler, for
they will help you climb to new heights.

Neck Exercises

I am a firm believer in neck training. I feel to be strong, the neck must be strong. When one thinks of cables you usually don't think of neck strength; however, there are actually many neck-developing exercises that can be performed with cables. I will share a handful of them with you. These exercises will quickly give you a stronger, more developed neck if you perform them correctly and consistently. I highly recommend these exercises for wrestlers and football players, but any-one interested in general development should perform at least one exer-cise that develops the back of the neck and one that works the front of the neck.

3.48   Rear Neck Forward Press

In performing this neck exercise, or any neck developer, start slowly with light tension. You will be waking up unused muscles if you haven't been training your neck on a regular basis. While performing neck exercises with the cables on the back of your head, you may wish to place a towel or cloth between your head and the cables for comfort.

You will find this first exercise a gold mine of strength for neck development. Start by placing your cables behind the back of your head. Grasp the handles with your palms down, at the sides of your head. From here, press straight forward with your arms, doing a forward press as your neck locks in place against the resistance. Be sure to keep your neck straight as your arms press forward. This exercise will build a great rear neck in record-breaking time. Be sure to start with light resistance at first. I would also suggest doing higher repetitions with neck exercises to get a good blood flow into the neck.

Muscles used: Rear neck, shoulders, triceps.

 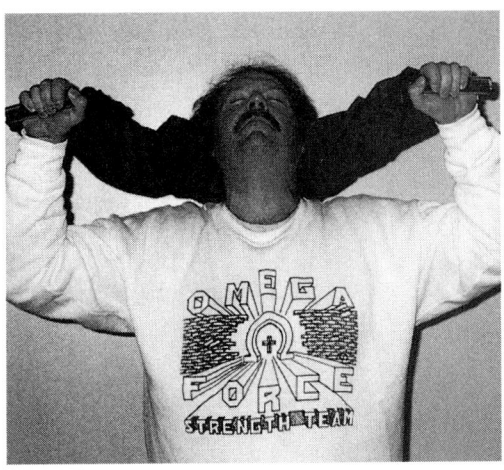

3.49   Rear Neck Pullback

Here is another cable exercise designed to develop the rear neck muscles. This exercise is similar to the last one, except the neck provides the range of motion instead of the arms. Start with the cables behind your head and the handles in front of you with the palms facing down. Press your cables forward so that your arms are straight in front of you. Hold this position throughout the exercise. Now pull your neck back and forth against the resistance of the cables. Perform this exercise until your neck is fatigued and has a good blood flow. This exercise is similar to training with a head strap with weight attached, but I believe you can develop a stronger neck with cables because of the steady pull applied against the neck; also the line of resistance seems to be more like that encountered in actual sports.

Muscles used: Rear neck, triceps, shoulders.

3.50   Rear Neck Overhead Press

This exercise is also a great rear neck developer. It works the neck at a different angle than the last two exercises did. Once again, begin with the cables against the back of your head. Your hands are holding the handles with your palms facing inward. From here, bend your head back and press the cables up into an overhead press. Keep your head back and resist the pull with your neck. Repeat the pressing movement until your neck is fatigued. You may wish to perform your overhead press with a slightly forward incline to prevent the cables from slipping.

Muscles worked: Rear neck, shoulders.

I have shown you three good cable exercises for building the rear neck muscles. I have many more, but I feel these three are plenty to get you started. From here, let's look at an excellent exercise for the front of the neck.

3.51   Front Neck Forward Pull

Here is a great neck developer for the front neck muscles. Start by grasping the handles with palms facing inward and placing the cables across your forehead; you may want to place a towel in between your head and the cables for comfort. Keep the cables stretched against your head throughout this exercise. Now move your neck back and forth against the resistance of the stretched cables. Use as much range of motion as possible without letting the cables slip. You will find that this exercise will give your front neck muscles a great pump.

Muscles worked: Front neck, shoulders.

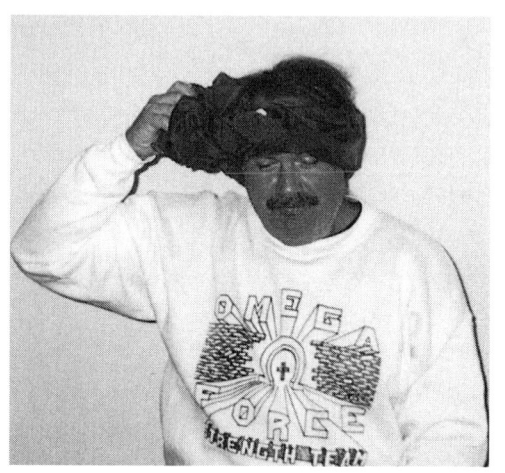
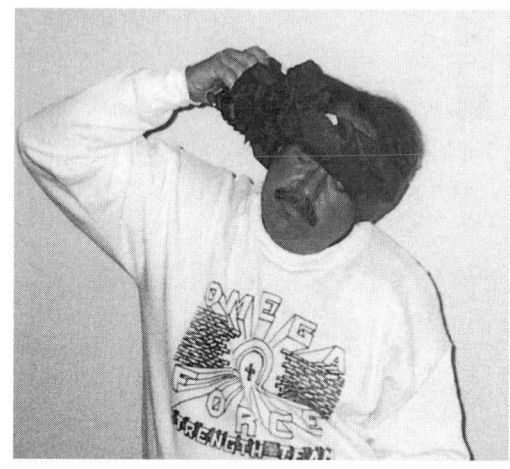

3.52   Side of Neck Pull

For complete neck development I have included the following exercise. Most people who train their necks regularly usually neglect the sides of their necks. These muscles are also very important for neck development. Place the middle of the cables against the side of your head, using a towel between your head and the cables if desired. Now bring the two handles together on the opposite side of your head. Grasp the two handles together with your hand and hold in place as you pull your head toward your shoulder against the resistance of the cables.
Be sure to pull with your neck in a straight line and do not twist your neck. Repeat this until fatigued, and then change sides and reverse the process so that each side of your neck is trained equally. Use a very light resistance on this exercise. You may find you are not very strong in this position. You will also find out that the muscles on the sides of your neck will gain strength very rapidly when trained in this fashion.

Muscles worked: Side of neck.

This concludes the exercises for the actual neck itself. Many people feel that by working the trapezius muscles they are working the actual neck muscles. I strongly disagree with this thinking. It is true that heavy trap work does slightly tie in to the neck. However, through many experiences, I have found that people who have huge, well-developed traps oftentimes have weak necks, and also that people with strong necks don't always have big traps. My point is that if you truly wish to develop a strong neck, you need to isolate the muscles with exercises like the ones I have mentioned in this section.

I do feel it is important to develop the surrounding areas of the neck, which of course are the traps. The traps are one of, if not the most, impressive-looking muscles on the body when properly developed. Let's look at some cable exercises that will develop these muscles.

3.53   Upright Row

The upright row is a very good weight training exercise that is used to develop bulk and strength. This great exercise can be done with cables as well. I can honestly say that you can work the trap region much better with cables than you can with weights. I found this out a few years ago when experimenting with the two different ways. The cables keep a steadier resistance throughout the entire movement.

You will experience a great blood flow into the traps with this cable exercise. Start by putting both feet fairly close together. From here, place one of your feet securely and firmly inside one handle, pinning it to the floor. Grasp the other handle with both hands. Keeping your back straight throughout the entire movement, pull the cables up to your chin with a slow, controlled movement. Return to the starting position and repeat until fatigued. Be sure to keep the pressure steady throughout the movement, with no jerking. I can guarantee that you will get the greatest pump in your traps with this movement.

Muscles worked: Traps and shoulders.

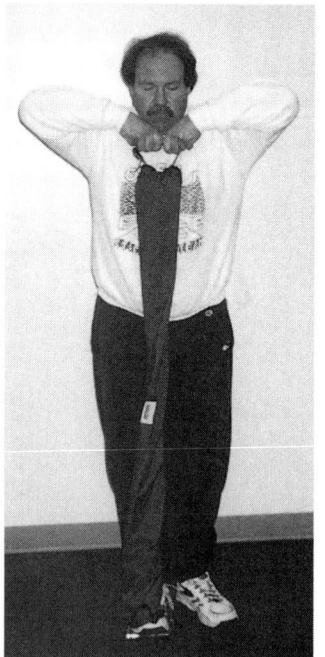

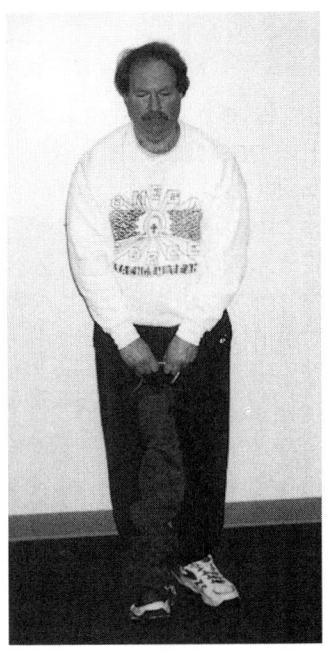

3.54   Shoulder Shrug

Another favorite trap builder is, of course, the shoulder shrug. The shrug is usually performed with a standard barbell. However, I feel that the range of motion is much better with dumbbells, for with dumbbells you are able to roll your shoulders, and you reap much better results. You should also get great results from cable shrugs because of the greater range of motion possible. Start by placing one foot well into one handle and securing it firmly to the floor. Now grasp the other handle with both of your hands and stretch the cables toward your head by rolling your shoulders upward toward your ears, actually trying to touch your ears. Repeat this shrugging process until fatigued. You can also work one side of your body at a time, using one hand, being sure to work both sides of your body equally.

Muscles worked: Trapezius muscles.

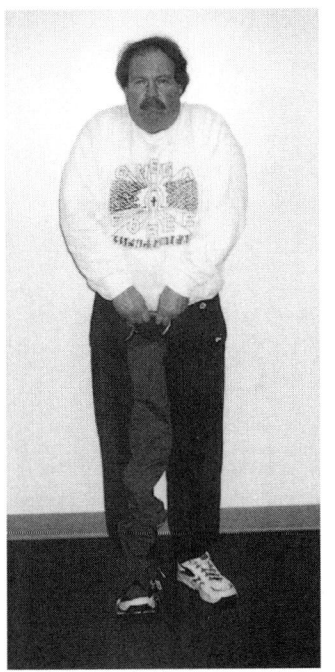

These are two basic, but effective exercises for developing the powerful trapezius muscles. You will find many of the basic cable exercises great for building the trap muscles as well; in fact, these muscles will probably become sore in the first few workouts by just doing the basic exercises. As I mentioned earlier, if you don't have any interest in developing the neck itself or the traps for your particular sport or goal, I would still suggest doing at least a couple of these exercises for general development. If you are a football player, or are involved in any combat sport, these are a must for survival. It would be safe to say that if your neck isn't strong, you're not strong.

Chapter 4

Questions
and
Answers

In this section I have answered some basic questions that usually arise when cables are used. It is natural to have questions about cable training, because there is not a lot of accessible instruction.

1. How many cables or how much resistance should you start with?

We touched on this question briefly in Chapter 3, Cable Exercises; however, I feel it is important to discuss it further. It is important at first to not be overly concerned with the number of cables or the amount of resistance you are using. The main objective at first is to get a good start at understanding and properly performing the exercises. Start very light at first and get a feel for the exercises. Experiment at first. If you feel your starting resistance is too light, gradually add resistance to the movement until it is enough. However, be careful not to go up too quickly, until your muscles get used to the exercises.

I have seen many people make the mistake of adding too much resistance too quickly. These people had enough strength to pull the cables at this setting, but their muscles were not yet used to the stresses cables put on their bodies. As a result, they pulled muscles and picked up nagging pains, usually in their shoulders or triceps. If you take it easy at first and let your muscles get used to the movements before you make huge jumps, you will reach great heights with your cable training.

2. How can I perform an exercise when I can't even get into the starting position?

It is true that some of the exercises can be difficult at first. In particular, people with large upper bodies have trouble getting the cables into some of the starting positions. If you have difficulty or cannot perform a certain exercise due to lack of flexibility, here are two suggestions. First of all, work on other cable exercises that increase flexibility; by doing similar exercises, you will dramatically increase flexibility.

My second suggestion, and probably the answer to most of your flexibility problems, comes from the following observation: I have found that often people cannot get the cables stretched into a certain position because they have too many cables for the exercise. There is too much pressure from the starting position for them to get the cables in the proper position. For example, in the back pressout, you may put yourself into a bind right from the start if you begin with too many cables. Therefore, if you are having difficulty, cut back on the number of cables or amount of resistance, and you may find the instant solution to your problem.

3. How safe is a cable set?

Years ago when cable pulling was so popular, the cables were mainly constructed of steel springs. These steel springs were very strong and durable. However, over a period of time, they would have a greater chance of breaking, due to the stress placed on them. As you could probably guess, these steel springs could be very dangerous when they broke. This is the reason why you don't hear of cable pulling much today. In these modern times, a company could not sell steel cables because of the danger involved. Therefore, cable sets were no longer sold, and cable pulling lost its popularity.

Today IronMind Enterprises, Inc. sells a competition set of cables which uses strong, high-grade surgical tubing instead of steel springs. As a result, you have a world-class cable set that is completely safe. You probably have noticed I mentioned that the cable set is a competition set. What I mean by this is that you can put more cables on this set than a human could ever pull. This results in unlimited size and strength for the puller.

These surgical tubing cables last for months before they break and then they can be used again. You should always keep your eye on the tubing for wear and tear; however when these cables do break, they usually just kind of fall to the side. For complete safety, IronMind has a sheath that fits over the cables to take away any chance of the cables' hitting you. This eliminates the chance of the cables' slapping you or someone else. This cable set is an absolute breakthrough in strength training, as well as safety.

4. What do you do when a cable breaks?

Many people would probably think, well, there goes one of my cables. After that, they probably throw the cable away. Actually, I occasionally like to see a cable break for the simple fact that this gives me an intermediate jump in resistance. In other words, when the cable breaks at the seam where it is attached, I then have a half cable, which has half the strength of the complete cable. This allows me to make lighter jumps in resistance, which on certain exercises is necessary to quickly progress. To use a broken cable, simply tie a loop into each end of the cable and hook the ends onto the handles where the attachment for the cables is. Now you have a cable which has half the resistance, which can be used to more easily and safely make jumps in resistance.

If you prefer the cable to be of the same resistance, all you have to do is tie the cable back together, forming a circle. This makes the cable the same as before. When tying a cable back together for its original strength, or for tying loops in both ends to make the resistance half-strength, be sure that you tie the cable securely. I would suggest that after you tie the cable, you pull it several times with your hands before you put it back on the cable set. This will ensure that you have tied the cables securely, and that they have tightened at the knots before you perform exercises with the reused cables. As you can see, you can make your cables last and last.

5. How am I doing compared to others in the different exercises?

First of all, try not to be too worried about poundage with your cables as long as you are improving using progressive resistance. To give you an idea, the cables from IronMind Enterprises are about 15 pounds of resistance per cable or, in other words, if you are performing one-handed curls with a pretty good stretch with five cables, you are curling about 75 pounds.

Another important point to make is that the farther the cables stretch, the more resistance is applied. So the taller a person is, or the longer the puller's arms are, the farther the cables are stretched. The end result is more resistance in the lockout position for the person with the greater wingspan. For example, a puller with short arms may perform an exercise with six cables attached, and a puller with long arms may perform the same exercise with five cables attached. The short-armed puller with six cables will experience greater resistance in the initial pull, but the longer-armed puller with five cables may experience just as much resistance in the final lockout position due to his longer wingspan. The main point to remember is to train consistently and progressively. As I mentioned earlier, little by little one goes far.

This section of questions and answers could go on and on. However, I feel there is one more point that must be made.

6. Are there are certain exercises that the cable length does not accommodate?

Some movements suffer because of improper range of motion. For example, the bow and arrow pull or the seated concentration curl cannot be performed with a good range of motion, because the cables usually are far too long for the exercise. Here is a simple answer to the problem. Simply double or overlap the cables so that they become half the length. Hook them back up to the handles and you now have a cable set that is half the length of the original set. Now you can perform exercises like the bow and arrow pull, the concentration curl, the one-arm row, and the one-handed deadlift with complete range of motion. As you can plainly see, cables are much more versatile than you ever imagined.

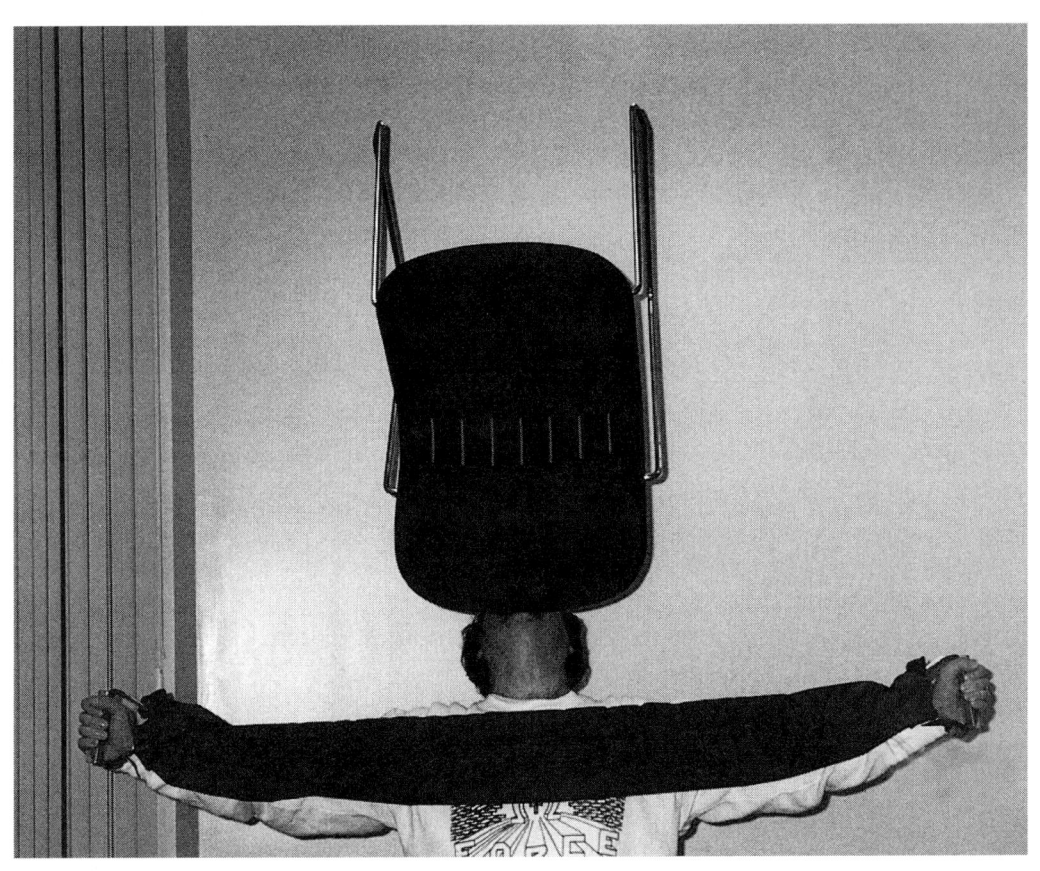

John Brookfield's idea of a balanced cable program—
or, as John says, "graduation exercises."

It would be safe to say that if your neck isn't strong, you're not strong.